ISRAELI OCCUPATION
International Law and Political Realities

by

DONALD E. GEORGE

Exposition Press Hicksville, New York

FIRST EDITION

Address inquiries to Exposition Press, Inc., 900 South Oyster Bay Road, Hicksville, NY 11801.

Library of Congress Catalog Card Number: 79-54671

ISBN 0-682-49439-9

Printed in the United States of America

Israeli Occupation

To the Palestinian people whose
lands are wrongfully held

Contents

Preface

I have often wondered whether or not anyone ever reads the preface to a book. In some instances, the preface can be one of the most important portions of the book, for it gives the reader an insight into the perspective and thinking of the author and assists the reader in understanding the style of the author. For instance, a reader of the late playwright George Bernard Shaw would find his prefaces far more lengthy, informative, and at times, far more amusing, than his actual plays.

In this case, the bulk of *Israeli Occupation: International Law and Political Realities* was written in the fall of 1973 in lieu of an examination in a law school course on international law. Its importance lay in analysis of facts and generally accepted principles of international law rather than in my expertise. At the same time, because my ethnic background is half Lebanese and half Tennessee hillbilly, it was relatively easy for me to attempt to put into practice the "professional objectivity" required of an American attorney.

After submission of the manuscript and its acceptance (much to my pleasure gradewise), the manuscript remained shelved for several years while I completed law school and attempted to set myself up in the private practice of law. The manuscript was read by friends all of whom recommended its publication. Yet, when one is not rich, famous, or in possession of some titillating piece of fact or fiction, publication is not an easy thing to bring about. However, through the generosity of certain clients who made efforts toward paying the legal fees which they incurred, the author was able to seek out and find a publisher.

During the years in which the manuscript languished, significant developments were taking place in the Middle East. The 1973 Yom Kippur War brought to world attention the necessity for finding a permanent solution to the Arab-Israeli problems which had resulted in four wars in twenty-five years. At the same time, the world recognized that one of the major stumbling blocks to peace in the Middle East was the question of the rights of the Palestinian people to a homeland and the demands by the Palestinians for such a homeland. This problem was further complicated by the fact that Jews immigrating from all parts of the world were being settled on lands captured during the 1967 war, lands to which the Palestinians laid claim. These settlements were being founded and increased despite the outcry of the Arab states and were in direct conflict with United Nations Security Council Resolution 242, which espoused the principle of nonrecognition of lands taken by conquest during war.

Continued Israeli occupation of the lands taken in 1967 and continued policies of settling immigrated Jews on what were formerly Arab lands have created a violent hostility toward them among the Palestinians and their leadership, the Palestinian Liberation Organization. PLO acts of terrorism throughout the world and raids from bases in Lebanon have resulted in Israeli reprisal raids into Lebanon. Repeated actions of raids and reprisals have resulted in a general civil war in Lebanon.

Lebanon is the truly unfortunate victim of the Middle East conflict between the Arabs and the Israelis. For many years, Lebanon was able to keep itself out of the conflict and remained the most stable country in the Middle East. It was the center for trade and business in the Middle East. Multinational corporations and financial institutions maintained their centers of operation in Beirut. Yet, the Lebanese government became entangled in disputes with the PLO over PLO raids into Israel and the Israeli reprisals. Now, the country of Lebanon lies in ruins, its economy devastated.

While the Palestinian people pressed for their rights to a homeland, another Arab leader was establishing his leadership role through numerous acts of political and personal courage.

Anwar Sadat had succeeded the very popular President Nasser as ruler of Egypt. At a time when his country's economy was on the verge of collapse, when Israelis were enlarging their influence over conquered territories through settlements, when world opinion seemingly ignored the plight of the Arabs, Sadat took it upon himself to bring the problems of the Middle East into the forefront with the 1973 Yom Kippur War, and upon failure to achieve a military victory, he took it upon himself to find a way to peace in the Middle East. It was Anwar Sadat who broke the barrier to peace by announcing that he would go to Israel and speak to the Knesset. That action brought a concentrated effort on the part of the leaders of both Egypt and Israel. Yet numerous barriers to peace remained. Israeli Prime Minister Begin found himself caught between his past rhetoric favoring the establishment of more Israeli settlements in the occupied territories and the opportunity to bring about peace in the Middle East.

The new impetus to the peace efforts came from someone outside traditional circles of politics, yet a man holding a most important political office, United States President Jimmy Carter. President Carter, responding to the disgust of the American people with traditional politicians and their hope that someone outside of Washington would effectively deal with American foreign policy, took it upon himself to act as mediator in the Arab-Israeli dispute. President Carter's efforts were focused on a summit meeting he had with President Sadat and Prime Minister Begin at Camp David in the Maryland mountains, which eventually resulted in a treaty of peace signed by the two nations on March 26, 1979.

Because of these developments, this manuscript, previously shelved, came back into light, and new chapters were added to reflect these developments.

Israel Occupation: International Law and Political Realities analyzes the actions taken by both sides, Israeli and Arab, in terms of international law. To the general reader, the term *international law* means a series of principles of conduct according to which nations should govern themselves when dealing with other nations. Most people, no matter what their origin or citizenship, are well aware of the fact that their conduct in their respective nations is governed by the laws of the nation in which they live. Those laws are enforceable by means of various sanctions or penalties. International law, in theory, operates in the same way. Nations are required to conduct themselves in accordance with principles. Those principles, or laws, come from past practice between nations and from dictates of responsible bodies such as the United Nations. Throughout this book, reference is made to United Nations Security Council Resolution 242. That resolution establishes the principle that nations can no longer annex lands conquered by war. This principle is totally opposite to the international practice acceptable during the nineteenth century, when boundaries changed frequently depending upon which nation won or lost what war. Now, the conquest of territories is no longer acceptable in international law, and the actions of the Israeli government are analyzed in light of this principle.

At the same time, the reader must be aware of political realities, whether he agrees or disagrees with what is actually going on. Prior to the treaty of peace between Egypt and Israel, political realities dictated that the Israelis had taken the lands during the 1967 war, that they were settling their citizens on those occupied territories, and that they would eventually annex those territories to the state of Israel. Under the terms of the treaty, however, Israel has agreed to withdraw both military and civilian persons from the lands taken from Egypt during the 1967 war. However, this is to be a phased withdrawal, which will take place over three years and will not begin for some ten months after the approval of the treaty by the two nations. The international community will look on with great interest at Israel's compliance with the withdrawal provisions of the treaty. If Israel does, in fact, withdraw, it will mark a distinct change in political realities, a change which could become the foundation of a just and lasting peace in the Middle East.

Finally, this book does not purport to be the final authority on the situation in the Middle East. Just as in the practice of law there are no purely black issues or purely white issues, but instead issues which are comprised of various shades of gray, so in the Middle East situation neither side is totally right. There is room for compromise on both sides. The question is the degree of compromise which is required. I invite discussion of the issues raised in this book, and I challenge the reader to think about what is being read, about the positions taken by the various sides on the issues, about the conclusions I have drawn. It is the independent thought, the free discussion, and the agreement on principles and the disagreement on concepts which lead to new ideas, ideas which may be helpful in assisting the parties in their efforts to resolve the Arab-Israeli conflict and to prevent further bloodshed and destruction.

1

International Law and Conflict Resolution

On September 24, 1973, United States Secretary of State Henry Kissinger, himself a winner of the Nobel Peace Prize for his part in ending American involvement in the Vietnam War, told the United Nations General Assembly, "We strive for a world in which the rule of law governs."[1] These words were well chosen, for the primary purpose of the United Nations is—to use the Charter's words: "to maintain international peace and security. . . ."[2] Thus the rule of law must replace the rule of force in conflict resolution.

This series of essays will examine the role of international law in the Arab-Israeli crisis, particularly in relation to the status of the lands which the Israelis conquered in the course of the Six-Day War of 1967 and continued to occupy following that war. No court is going to hand down a legal decision resolving the conflict over the status of those lands. The International Court of Justice would seem the logical arbiter, but both sides to the Arab-Israeli conflict seriously restricted the scope of litigable issues in accepting compulsory jurisdiction. Thus, a case between the two parties was impossible.[3] Yet although there was no actual legal solution and despite the fact that the Israelis remained in occupation of those lands, this series of essays should not be considered an academic exercise, for it is useful to have governments know that their activities will be subjected to examination by international legal scholars who will judge the legality of their actions.[4]

Isaac Shapiro, a member of the New York Bar, noted at the Thirteenth Annual Hammarskjöld Forum that "Some years before his death the late General Douglas MacArthur said that: 'War is no longer a feasible arbiter.' It is time that the truth of this statement as to the impracticability of military solutions be acknowledged and the Middle East dispute be resolved in a peaceful manner, one which will advance the use of law in the settlement of disputes."[5] Once again, if the impracticability of military solutions is to be acknowledged, international disputes must be settled by the use of international law.

International law has traditionally been viewed as consisting of an existing network of legal relationships among nations. The Statute of the International Court of Justice views those relationships as being based on treaties, customary international law, the general principles of law recognized by civilized nations, and the writings of qualified authorities. The Charter of the United Nations and the decisions of the International Court of Justice and of other competent international tribunals are also considered to be major sources of modern international law.[6]

A noted civil law maxim states, *Narra mihi facta narabo tibi jus:* Law does not operate in a vacuum, or in the abstract, but only in the closest contact with facts. Moreover, the merit of legal exposition depends directly upon the relationship with the facts. However, in order to adequately analyze and to apply the international law which is applicable to the Arab-Israeli crisis, there must first be an analysis of the facts surrounding the controversy. As the reader will see shortly, it is in the interpretation of these facts that much of the controversy lies. Each side interpreted differently the facts and events leading up to the 1967 war and the subsequent Israeli occupation of Arab territories. Each based his political position and arguments for that position upon his individual interpretation of those facts. In order to get a complete view of the controversy, one must make an independent analysis of the facts surrounding the controversy and a critical analysis of the arguments advanced by each side.

2

The One-Sided Perspective

One of many interesting aspects of the Jewish culture is that it requires moral justification for military and political acts. This moral justification must be in terms of social justice, where justice means humanist ethics.[1] The vehicle for the determination of moral justification is international law, and as was mentioned earlier, the application of international law requires an analysis of the applicable facts. Therefore, the media have played a major role in the Arab-Israeli conflict, a role controlled largely by the Israelis.

Perhaps Israel's greatest achievement was, not its smashing military victory in the 1967 Six-Day War, but instead its success in communicating its point of view—for control of the social institution of mass communication is a major component of power. Thus, the campaign to present the Israeli version, and only the Israeli version, of what was happening in the Middle East in the summer of 1967 was without comparison in its extent and intensity.[2] This type of campaign is exemplified by Israel's massive efforts to indict Egypt as the aggressor of the 1967 war before any facts were presented, even though it was Israel who had actually started the shooting.[3]

The domination of the Israeli point of view is particularly noteworthy in examining American press coverage of the Arab-Israeli conflict. The most striking element was (and continued to be) the extreme reluctance of the American press to criticize Israel or its actions, even on the editorial page or in feature articles. Whenever Israel struck at its Arab neighbors, mistreated

the Arab population in the Arab territories it occupied militarily after 1967, or annexed portions of that territory, such actions were justified, and Israeli arguments were presented as proof of the logic and rightness of the situation. Moreover, Israeli achievements seem beyond compare according to "authoritative" reports about how the Israelis "made the desert bloom." These reports were used to justify Israeli annexation of certain Arab territories captured during the 1967 war, and they bring to mind similar arguments of colonialists which had supposedly been rejected by Western liberals some twenty years before.[4]

This pattern of attitudes and sympathies which was manifested by the American press fostered almost complete identification with the people of Israel. The Arabs, meantime, were reduced to little more than caricatures.[5] Whereas the Israelis were being portrayed as practically without fault, rarely, if ever, were any good qualities attributed to the Arabs.[6] Israel was seen as a Western state populated by technology-minded, energetic, democratic, pioneering frontiersmen who are transforming a wilderness and providing a home for the persecuted. The Arab states, on the other hand, were seen as exasperatingly inscrutable, unreliable, inept, backward, authoritarian, and emotional. Israel was our staunch friend and ally. The Arabs, meantime, threw stones at American embassies.[7]

In this context, even when the Arab point of view is presented, it sounds strange and unconvincing to the reader or the listener. This is, again, because the audience was so saturated with a pro-Israeli viewpoint that it unquestioningly rejected anything contrary to that stance. Another tactic used to discredit the Arab position was to let the "Communists" speak for the Arabs. This tactic is exemplified by a June 18, 1967, *New York Times* article, which reproduced excerpts from *Izvestia,* one of the two main newspapers of the Soviet Union (the other being *Pravda*). The *Izvestia* article denounced the Israelis as aggressors. At about the same time, *Time* magazine dismissed reports of looting and acts of atrocity by Israeli soldiers as a "Communist charge."[8]

The most important reason for the treatment the Israelis

received from the American press and people is the fact that the Israelis are Jews. This fact alone endows sympathy for Israel with all the sanctity of rejection of mass extermination and disavowal of country-club bigotry. American liberals, it seems, could not find fault with a collective Jewish cause because doing so would carry an immediate implication of anti-Semitism. Consequently, support for Israel was an automatic liberal cause, and actions by Israel that would have drawn strong condemnations if undertaken by another country were defended by liberals with the same arguments that had earlier been used by those advocating such causes as colonialism and racial inequality.[9]

In more abstract terms, the danger of such one-sided reporting of only the Israeli position can best be expressed by an old French proverb: *Une bonne conscience est un doux oreiller*, which means, "An easy, tranquil conscience is a soft pillow." That is to say that when one is resting on a soft pillow, sleep comes easily and one's dreams obscure reality. So too in real life, one can be blinded by one's hopes and aspirations, particularly in relation to the methods employed to achieve those dreams. In other words, one may fail to see the sufferings he causes others in the attainment of his particular dream, while justifying even the most detestable of his own acts by saying that since his goal is essentially good and just, any means taken to accomplish that goal are also good and just[10]—in short, Machiavelli's infamous, "the end justifies the means."

Later, however, there was an effort on the part of the world press to give a fair accounting of the Arab viewpoint. This change was noted by Egyptian Information Minister Dr. Muhammed Abd al-Qadir Hatim in a press conference on January 22, 1973: "Immediately before 1967 and until 1972 Israel succeeded in misleading the world public by pretending to be a lover of peace and by pretending to be a weak party. Due to their honest stand, the free press and honest information media contributed to exposing the real ambitions of Israel and explained to the world public that Israel is a racist and expansionist state based on aggression." This change in the attitude of the world

public was due to Israel's insistence on retaining the lands captured in the 1967 war, which the Israelis had continued to occupy.[11] The American press, on the other hand, maintained their pro-Israeli stance in regards to Israeli settlement of Arab lands by regarding that settlement as illustrative of the Israeli "pioneering spirit."[12]

In examining the Israeli diplomatic position in regards to the Arab-Israeli conflict, it is imperative that the reader be aware of the Israeli influence over the communications media. The Israeli stance in the early seventies was based mainly upon the arguments they had put forth in their propaganda campaign of 1967—arguments which, although they have been proven false, have not been closely examined because of the extensive influence the Israelis hold over the communications media. In this series of essays, the arguments the Israelis have used to justify their position will be examined in relation to international law, and many of the fallacies of their position will be pointed out.

3

Why Is It Important Who Started the 1967 War?

It is imperative at this point that the reader recall Israel's massive campaign in 1967, through its extensive control and influence over the media, to blame Egypt for the eruption of hostilities in June 1967, which led to Israeli occupation of the Sinai peninsula, the Golan Heights, and the Gaza Strip. The importance of this campaign to place the blame on Egypt lay in Israel's attempt to justify its continued occupation of those lands in terms of international law. I. L. Kenen, executive vice-chairman of the American-Israeli Public Affairs Committee, summed up the Israeli position when he said: "We should resist Arab pressures which call for Israel's total withdrawal from territories occupied in the six day war. There is nothing sacred about the 1967 frontiers and there is nothing rational about the demand that Israel withdraw to them. Israel *did not start* the war of 1967 and those who began the war and lost it cannot claim to reinstate the vantage points from which they initiated their aggression and from which they may resume it."[1] (Emphasis added.) Thus, Israel claimed her actions in 1967 were totally defensive. She claimed that since those actions in 1967 were defensive, her continued occupation of those Arab territories captured in 1967 was totally justified in terms of international law.[2]

Although international law does not give weight of recognition to conquests, as such, it does allow and give weight to any defensive action which is reasonably required to insure that

bordering lands will not again be used for aggressive purposes.[3] Where such defensive action results in the military capture and occupation of enemy territory belonging to the enemy sovereign, the occupation is justified under international law, and the occupying state is termed a legal occupant. The benefits of this status are numerous. First, the legal occupant is entitled to international recognition of the validity of his occupation until such time as a peace treaty with the ousted sovereign is signed. With a peace treaty, the lawful occupant is entitled to sovereignty over any lands which may be ceded to him. In the absence of a peace treaty, the lawful occupant can still acquire sovereignty over an occupied territory if he can effect either a debellatio, that is, a complete collapse of the enemy coupled with subjugation, traditionally exercised through annexation, or by prescription, which is a state of occupation remaining continuous, uninterrupted, and peaceful, provided that all other interested and affected parties have acquiesced in this exercise of authority.[4] These are the rights Israel claimed in attempting to justify her continued occupation of the Arab territories seized in 1967.

However, if it can be shown that Israel did not act in self-defense in 1967, but was instead the aggressor—as the Arabs have charged since 1967—then the status of Israel in terms of international law changes drastically. As Julius Stone, a noted professor of international law at the University of Sydney, Australia, has pointed out, "Whether belligerent occupation has been established depends not merely on the will of the belligerent, but on whether his actual control satisfies the standards of range and stability laid down by international law. If it does not, he is a mere invader enjoying a comparatively narrow legal authority.[5] Thus, according to Professor Stone, if a nation was not justified in using force under international law, that nation would not be entitled to assert any rights over conquered territories, since its status in international law is that of a "mere invader." This equitable principle forbidding states to acquire any legal right from a unilateral act not in accordance with international law is called *ex injuria jus non oritur,* and it was

applied many times by the Permanent Court of International Justice, which operated under the old League of Nations.

Under this doctrine, the unlawful invader-occupant is denied both international recognition of the lawfulness of his continued occupation and the capacity to acquire sovereignty. Oppenheim points out that "When the act alleged to be creative of a new [territorial right] is in violation of an existing rule of customary or conventional International Law. . . . the act in question is tainted with invalidity and is incapable of producing legal results beneficial to the wrongdoer in the form of new title or otherwise."[6] It is important to note, however, that the invalidity of an invader-occupant's presence can be negated and the rights of sovereignty over the occupied lands restored to him if the international community treats the illegal acquisition as a valid one.[7]

In the case of the Arab-Israeli confrontation, two things must be examined in order to determine the status of the Israeli occupation of Arab territories. First, the events leading up to the Six-Day War must be analyzed to determine if Israel is a lawful occupier or an invader-occupier, for, as has been shown, there is a substantial difference between the two classifications, particularly as to "rights of occupation." Second, if, as the Arabs have claimed, Israel was an invader-occupier, the position of the world community must be ascertained to determine if they have acquiesced to the "legality" of the occupation, in which case Israel would be entitled to the rights and privileges of a lawful occupier.

4

Who Really Started the 1967 War? A Look at Both Sides

Article 2, section 4, of the Charter of the United Nations states, "All members shall refrain in their international relations from the threat or use of force against the territorial integrity or political independence of any state, or in any other manner inconsistent with the purposes of the United Nations." On the other hand, article 51 states, in part, "Nothing in the present Charter shall impair the inherent right of individual or collective self-defense if an armed attack occurs against a Member of the United Nations." Therefore, it is a violation of the United Nations Charter for one member state to attack another member state, yet the Charter also recognizes a state's "inherent right" of "individual or collective self-defense."

In the early morning of June 5, 1967, the Israeli Air Force knocked out several Arab military airfields, and large-scale hostilities broke out.[1] Yet from the very beginning of the Six-Day War, Israel claimed to have been attacked first and set out on a massive propaganda campaign to indict Egypt as the aggressor before any facts were presented.

Israel, meantime, knew of the presence of an eyewitness whose proof could have been irrefutable. The U.S.S. *Liberty*, an electronics surveillance ship, was stationed off the coast of Israel in international waters. The ship's job was to monitor Israel air sorties, and it could have provided the data that might have branded Israel as the aggressor—in contravention to her vast propaganda campaign to put that brand upon Egypt. Had Israel

been proven the aggressor, she would have been deprived of the fruits of her victory. Unfortunately for the Arab states, Israel destroyed that evidence when she bombed and strafed the upper decks of the vessel where the equipment and collected data were stored. In addition to the destruction of the intelligence-gathering equipment, the Israeli attack killed 34 American sailors and wounded 166. A U.S. Navy board of inquiry concluded that the attack was deliberate and unprovoked. Although Israel claimed that it mistook the American vessel for an Egyptian one, the board of inquiry concluded that the Israeli planes and torpedo boats could not have failed to identify the ship as an American vessel in international waters and that the attack was intentional. Israel paid the United States $3,000,000 in damages and continued her propaganda campaign to brand Egypt as the aggressor and to claim she had been defending herself against an armed attack under article 51 of the United Nations Charter.[2]

Even months later—when, in consolidating the territories she occupied, Israel was freely admitting that she had been the first party to resort to the actual use of armed force in the 1967 war—she still attempted to justify that use as defensive under article 51. Israel attempted to justify her preemptive strike by asserting the "cumulative effect" of Egyptian actions prior to the 1967 war. These actions included the closing of the Straits of Tiran, which cut off passage through the Gulf of Aqaba; the ejection of the United Nations Emergency Force from their positions along the Sinai peninsula and the massing of Egyptian forces along the Egyptian-Israeli border; Egypt's signing of joint defense pacts with other nations, creating the fear of imminent destruction within Israel and leading the Israeli cabinet to support a preemptive strike; and the saber-rattling war fever generated in the streets of Cairo. Such a situation was deemed by Israel to be an "armed attack" under article 51 of the United Nations Charter.[3]

A careful examination of the events Israel claimed made her fear for her existence and which justified her preemptive strike may lead the reader to a different interpretation than that the Israeli cabinet used to approve their preemptive strike. Again,

the reader must remember that for quite some time the Israelis had the world believing that Egypt had "cast the first stone" in the Six-Day War, although this was later proven to be false.

Looking first to the Egyptian closing of the Straits of Tiran as a casus belli, even Allen Gerson, a staunch supporter of Israel and her diplomatic position, admits that closure of the straits was not in itself sufficient justification for initiating a general war under the terms of the United Nations Charter.[4] Israel claimed that the closing of the Straits of Tiran had seriously affected her economy. Yet the *New York Times* of June 5, 1967, noted that only one Israeli vessel had attempted to pass through the straits in the two preceding years, and it had been successful.[5] Moreover, the blockade was never actually put into effect, as evidenced by the passage of a German freighter through the straits to the Israeli port of Eilat.[6] At the time of the Israeli attack, Egypt had not stopped any vessel of any kind going through the Straits of Tiran to the Israeli port of Eilat. Furthermore, less than 10 percent of Israel's imports came through this strait.[7] Yet somehow these facts were "overlooked" by the Israeli cabinet. However, even if the blockage of the straits had served as a significant form of economic pressure, recourse to war would not have been justified under international law, for no degree of coercion employing the political, ideological, or economic instruments of foreign policy justifies recourse to military force.[8]

Israel's second point of justification for her preemptive strike against Egypt in 1967 was the forced departure from Sinai of the United Nations Emergency Force, which had been there since 1957, and the massing of Egyptian troops along the Egyptian-Israeli border. Several months later, Haim Bar-Ler, who was deputy chief of staff of the armed forces in 1967 (and would be Israeli minister of commerce and industry by 1973), admitted that the entrance of the Egyptians into Sinai was not a casus belli.

Egypt's President Nasser had explained that his motive for asking the United Nations Emergency Force to leave and for massing troops along Israel's borders was to dissuade Israel from

continuing its reprisal policies against Syria,[9] a countermeasure which is justified under international law.[10] Moreover, under the terms of the United Nations Charter, permission of the Egyptian government was required in order for the Emergency Force to operate on its soil—permission which could be withdrawn at any time. This permission is required because a state's sovereignty and integrity forbid the entry of foreign forces, even those which are international in composition and character, into its territory without its voluntary approval, unless such forces are dispatched by the Security Council for enforcement actions taken under Chapter VII of the United Nations Charter.[11]

Israel had also claimed that the massing of Egyptian troops along her border had made her fear for her very existence because of the war fever being generated in the streets of Cairo.[12] Near the end of May 1967, however, Nasser had begun to deescalate the Egyptian military presence along the Sinai peninsula, and on May 30, 1967, he had declared at a press conference that the United Arab Republic did not want a war with Israel and had suggested that the Palestine Mixed Armistice Commission be revived to supervise a phased withdrawal of Egyptian and Israeli forces from the armistice lines. He had further offered to take the question of the Straits of Tiran to the International Court of Justice for adjudication.[13]

Had Israel truly feared for her existence, as she claimed, she could have allowed the United Nations Emergency Force to simply cross the border into Israel. This Israel consistently refused to do, maintaining the "integrity of her soil. However, as the Arabs had been saying, there was no threat to the survival of Israel in the days leading up to the 1967 war. Matityahu Peled, the Israeli Army's quartermaster general in the 1967 war, admitted that the survival argument was a bluff which was born and developed after the war."[14]

Israel, however, remained "proud" of the fact that she had not been branded the "aggressor" in the 1967 war.[15] Yet the facts that most of the information concerning the war came from the media and that the Israeli government conducted huge campaigns to put the blame on Egypt for the start of the 1967

war while claiming its actions to be "solely" in "self-defense" could have been responsible for the United Nations not putting any blame on Israel.[16]

In light of Israel's bluff that her security was endangered and her propaganda campaign to blame Egypt for the outbreak of war in 1967, it becomes important to take a second look at the Arabs' charge of aggression on the part of Israel. A report to the Pentagon in Washington shortly before the outbreak of the 1967 war contained detailed information concerning military strengths and weaknesses of the two sides, and it showed that Israel's military superiority was indisputable. Based on this report, Pentagon analysts submitted another report to President Lyndon Johnson which correctly forecast the events of the 1967 war.

On the basis of both Israel's military superiority and her own knowledge of that superiority, Georgetown Professor of Government Hisham Sharabi concluded:

> It is not surprising that President Nasser's signaled promises—withdrawal of troops, adjudication of the Aqaba question, political settlement of outstanding issues were ignored. From Israel's standpoint, the anticipated rewards of military action certainly exceeded those of diplomatic negotiations. Israel acted not spontaneously in fear or in anger, but calmly, in the light of careful calculations based on extensive intelligence and highly sophisticated analysis of the overall political and military.[17]

Should Professor Sharabi's thesis prove true, Israel violated Article 2, Section 4, of the United Nations Charter and committed an act of aggression—defined by the Rio Pact (the Inter-American Treaty of Reciprocal Assistance of 1947), which has the only binding definition of aggression, as being:

> *a*) unprovoked armed attack by a state against the territory, the people, or the land, sea, or air forces of another state; *b*) Invasion, by the armed forces of a state, of the territory of (another) state, through the trespassing of boundaries demarcated in accordance with a treaty, judicial decision or arbitral award, or, in the absence of frontiers thus demarcated, invasion affecting a region which is under effective jurisdiction of another state.[18]

Moreover, under international law, a state which has committed an act defined as aggressive cannot assert a claim of self-defense to cover its illegal activities.[19]

After examining from the Arab viewpoint the Israeli Air Force attack on the early morning of June 5, 1967, against Egyptian air bases, it is evident that this attack was but one of a series of Israeli reprisals[20] against her Arab neighbors—perhaps for "guerrilla activities," perhaps for other reasons, including the desire to conquer territories to which she claimed a "historical right."[21] The series of attacks began on July 14, 1966, with an Israeli air attack on Syrian territory. This was followed by the seemingly senseless attack on the village of Al-Sammū', Jordan, on November 13, 1966. On April 7, 1967, the Israeli Air Force carried its "reprisal" to such lengths that it bombed near Damascus.[22] In addition, plans for a further Israeli attack were discovered by a *New York Times* correspondent in Tel Aviv, a plan which Nasser learned of through Syrian intelligence officers. Information about troop movements in accordance with that plan were corroborated by Lebanese sources.[23]

Moreover, Israel was openly threatening to attack Syria again. On May 15, 1967, Israeli Prime Minister Levi Eshkol told an interviewer that Israel was ready to make a lightning military strike against Syria—powerful enough to effect a change of heart by the government in Damascus and quick enough to prevent any other countries from rallying to Syria's aid.[24] He declared that "We shall hit them when, where and how we choose."[25] The actions taken by Egyptian President Nasser, which were later used by Israel to justify her preemptive strike, can now be seen in a different light.

Therefore, in light of the examination of the facts leading up to the 1967 war, three conclusions are in order. First, Israel was in no danger of attack from the Arab states, as she has claimed. Egyptian President Nasser had stated publicly that he would not attack Israel and had assured Secretary-General U Thant and the United Nations that he "would not initiate offensive action against Israel,"[26] a fact that the late President Lyndon B. Johnson noted in his memoirs. Moreover, even as late

as June 4, 1967, United States Special Envoy to Cairo, Charles Yost, concluded, ". . . there does not seem to have been any intention in Cairo to initiate a war."[27] The British had similarly been assured that Egypt would not attack. In addition, there is ample indication that Israel's intelligence services knew for sure that Egypt was not going to attack.[28]

The second conclusion to be reached at this point is that prior to the Israeli preemptive strike of June 5, 1967, Israel was in no danger of being exterminated, as she has claimed to have been. Adman Al-Pachachi, minister of state of the United Arab Emirates, reminded the members of the Security Council of the United Nations that "Until the outbreak of the 1967 war, Israel had never complained about the so-called vulnerability and insecurity of the armistice lines. Quite the contrary, it considered them highly satisfactory. . . ."[29] Furthermore, in a debate published June 10, 1972, in the daily newspaper of the Israeli Labor party, Israeli generals Weizman, Gavich, Peled, and Herzog all agreed on one point—*no* danger of extermination had threatened Israel before it launched its preemptive strike.[30] In fact, individuals who had been members of the Israeli cabinet during the Six-Day War were saying by 1973 that the story of the threat of extermination had been invented by Israel after the war to justify her continued occupation and annexation of the occupied Arab territories.[31]

The third and final conclusion that can be drawn at this point is that Israel's preemptive strike of June 5, 1967, cannot be justified as an action of self-defense under the terms of article 51 of the United Nations Charter. Dr. John Lawrence Hargrove, director of studies for the American Society of International Law, indicated that "[I]n our premordial international community, an exception to the prohibition of violence that legitimizes such a first strike would make the world a substantially more dangerous place in which to live and this is not the sort of world envisaged in the United Nations Charter. So far as I am aware Israel stands alone among governments in espousing her position on that point."[32] Thus, it is the general consensus within the international community that an armed attack is

required against a state in order to justify her use of military force under article 51 of the United Nations Charter. The Charter was intended to repudiate the notion that imminent threat of force authorizes preemptive use of force in self-defense, in order to reduce the number of opportunities for conflict to begin because of a nation's jumping the gun. Hence, the preemptive strike of Israel against Egypt on the morning of June 5, 1967, cannot be justified under international law.[33] Since Israel's attack was illegal in terms of international law, her position would seem to have been that of an invader-occupant, with few rights at all and no right of sovereignty (as mentioned in chapter 3). Under international law, therefore, Israel should withdraw her forces from occupied Arab lands.[34]

Israeli Occupation

5

Security Council Resolution 242 and International Law

The Arab-Israeli conflict has been a bitter one, and genuine rights are involved on both sides. Resolution 242, adopted by the United Nations Security Council on November 22, 1967, outlined the most feasible settlement[1] and has been considered by the overwhelming majority of United Nations member states as the international legal foundation for a Middle East settlement.[2] A settlement based on this resolution was acceptable to the great powers,[3] and it is difficult to see how there could be a satisfactory settlement of the problems in the Middle East except on the basis of the principles on which Resolution 242 is based.

Resolution 242 was taken from the British draft and represented a compromise between the Soviet and American drafts of the resolution. The Soviet draft required the Security Council to urge that "the parties to the conflict should immediately withdraw to the positions they held before 5 June 1967," in accordance with the principle that the seizure of territories as the result of war is inadmissible. The American draft, on the other hand, contained neither the statement of the principle forbidding the acquisition of territory by war nor the requirement of withdrawal to the boundaries held before 5 June 1967.[4] The British resolution, a compromise between these two stands, included the principle of the inadmissibility of acquisition of territory by war, but required the withdrawal to be a part of the complete settlement rather than a condition for negotiation.[5] The resolution was adopted under Chapter 6, Article 37, of the United Nations Charter.[6]

One of the major differences between the diplomatic positions of the Arabs and the Israelis centered on their different interpretations of Security Council Resolution 242 and of whether the resolution calls for withdrawal of Israeli troops from all the territories captured in 1967 and occupied afterward, or only from some of them. Israel maintained that the resolution only calls for withdrawal from some of the territories, to be determined by direct negotiations between the parties. The Arabs, meantime, refused to negotiate directly with the Israelis and called for withdrawal from *all* the territories, in accordance with the preamble of the resolution, which emphasizes the "inadmissibility of the acquisition of territory by war."[7] Since each side could interpret Resolution 242 to its individual advantage and they were unable to settle their differences as to interpretation, the resolution failed to be the foundation for peace in the Middle East.[8]

Israel's position that Resolution 242 requires withdrawal from only some, and not all, of the territories, was based upon the wording of the resolution, which specifies withdrawal from "territories" occupied since 1967 rather than "the territories" occupied since 1967. Thus, the fact that the word *the* does not appear in relation to *territories* was felt to be most significant. The Israelis noted also that repeated attempts in the Security Council to insert the word *the* before the word *territories* had failed.[9] Moreover, they pointed out that the word *all* also does not appear in connection with *territories,* and that this, too, was significant. They concluded that the omission of the words *the* and *all* justified their interpretation of Resolution 242.

Hence, they interpreted Resolution 242 as allowing their annexation of East Jerusalem and as making the states of the Golan Heights, captured from Syria, and of Sharm El-Sheikh and the Gaza Strip, conquered from Egypt, nonnegotiable. Unable to win peace after winning three wars in twenty years, Israel was determined to retain the new military advantages brought about by her conquest of these Arab territories. These new territories created a security line far removed from the heart of Israel.[10] Israel's position was best summed up by its foreign minister, Josef Tekoah. When speaking before the Security Council in 1973, he said:

> The purpose of Resolution 242 is to establish a new situation and not to restore the one created by the provisional military armistice lines, a situation of vulnerability and peril that resulted in the 1967 hostilities. It is clear that the "secure and recognized boundaries" are not defined in the resolution, being dependent upon negotiation and agreement. There is no rule or principle in international law preventing agreed border changes in peace treaties even when recognized boundaries exist. Israel's acceptance of the November, 1967, resolution has been and is based on that assumption.[11]

The Arabs viewed the Israeli position as that of a victor seeking to annex territories from the conquered countries.[12] They themselves emphasized the preamble of the resolution, which forbids the acquisition of territory by war, and they consequently demanded the complete withdrawal of Israeli troops from *all* occupied territory.[13] Any other interpretation would have amounted to justifying the acquisition of territory by force, in contravention to international law, which states that military supremacy cannot create new rights where none existed previously.[14] Seen in this light, Resolution 242 demands the immediate and unconditional withdrawal of Israeli forces of occupation from all the territories they occupied and Israeli affirmation of the sanctity of international borders.[15]

The Arabs saw the Israeli interpretation of the words "secure and recognized boundaries" in Resolution 242 as an attempt to build on those words an illegitimate theory from which to obtain a license for territorial expansion. Reemphasizing the inadmissibility of the acquisition of territory by war, the Arabs asserted that the territorial expansion the Israelis seek is prohibited both by the terms of the Charter and by the terms of Resolution 242.[16]

In addition to citing the preamble in support of their position, the Arabs referred to paragraph 1 (ii) of the resolution, which affirms the principle of "respect for and acknowledgment of the sovereignty. . . . territorial integrity . . . and political independence of every state in the area. . . ." They contended that no state could possibly consider her territorial integrity acknowledged and respected if another state had forcibly occupied her territories and refused to withdraw from them. According to this line of reasoning, the permanent loss of any territory by any state as a consequence of the June 1967 war would constitute a violation of Resolution 242.[17]

Arab leaders recognized that Resolution 242 required major concessions on their part, and they accepted those concessions. The resolution requires them to give up positions which they have held onto for twenty years as matters of principle. These positions to be given up included (1) refusal to recognize the state of Israel and to end the state of belligerency; (2) refusal to grant Israeli shipping the right to use the Suez Canal; (3) refusal to permit freedom of access for shipping bound for the Israeli port of Eilat through the Straits of Tiran.[18]

Lord Caradon, Foreign Minister of Great Britain and the principal architect of the British draft that was to become Resolution 242, stated the British position in a February 10, 1973, interview, saying,

> Withdrawal should take place to secure and recognized boundaries, and these words were very carefully chosen: they have to be secure and they have to be recognized. They will not be secure unless they are recognized. And that is why one has to work for agreement. If we had attempted to draw a map, we would have been wrong. We did not. And I would defend absolutely what we did. It was not for us to lay down exactly where the border should be. I know the 1967 border very well. It is not a satisfactory border; it is where troops had to stop in 1947, just where they happened to be that night. That is not a permanent boundary.[19]

Although this position might seem to add support to the Israeli point of view, nonetheless, the fact remains that the resolution also took into account the principle of the inadmissibility of the acquisition of territory by means of war.

This principle was also acknowledged by the interpretation given Resolution 242 by the Soviet Union. They saw the principle that an aggressor has no right to any territorial reward for his aggression as a generally recognized principle of modern international law. Under this interpretation of Resolution 242, Israeli troops were required to withdraw from all of the Arab lands occupied since 1967.[20]

The United States interpretation of the resolution avoided any mention of the preamble and seemed, in fact, to discount it —stating that the resolution neither endorses nor precludes extension of Israel's border beyond the boundaries held before 5 June 1967.[21] The United States interpretation connected withdrawal of Israeli armed forces with "termination of all claims or states of belligerency and respect for and acknowledgment of the sovereignty, territorial integrity and political independence of every state in the area and their right to live in peace within secure and recognized boundaries free from threats or acts of force."[22]

Resolution 242 of the United Nations Security Council rests upon several fundamental principles under the United Nations Charter. The first principle recognizes the territorial integrity of states. A state is deprived of its territorial integrity whenever any part of its territory is forceably detached, for whatever alleged reason. Moreover, in regard to withdrawal, the resolution concerns itself with Arab as well as Israeli security and does not support the idea of Israeli security at the expense of Arab security.[23]

Another fundamental principle appears in the preamble to Resolution 242: the inadmissibility of the acquisition of territory by war. This principle goes beyond the principle of "no fruits of aggression." It says that there shall be no territorial gains from war, meaning the use of considerable armed force. Thus, its application to the 1967 Arab-Israeli conflict would necessitate Israel's withdrawal from the occupied Arab territories, whether or not she was the aggressor.[24]

The inadmissibility of the acquisition of territory by war was accepted as a principle of American international law in the form "no title by conquest" in 1878 at the Pan American Conference. It was reaffirmed in the Buenos Aires Declaration of

1936, the Lima Declaration of 1938, and the Bogota Charter of the Organization of American States in 1948.

This principle was one which was assumed in President Woodrow Wilson's famous Fourteen Points, and it was applied in Europe in the peace settlements of World War I by requiring plebiscites to justify any territorial transfer. This principle was also assumed by the League of Nations as a necessary implementation of the League Covenant's guarantee of the territorial integrity of all members. The United States insisted that this principle be followed in 1932 when, in the Stimson Doctrine, she refused to recognize any acquisitions by Japan from its invasion and military occupation of Manchuria.[25]

In addition to its incorporation in Security Council Resolution 242, the principle of the inadmissibility of the acquisition of territory by war is embodied in other fundamental United Nations documents, such as the Declaration on the Strengthening of International Security and the Declaration on Principles of Friendly Relations among States.[26] The principle was reaffirmed by Security Council Resolutions 252 (1968), 267 (1969), and 298 (1971) and by General Assembly Resolutions 2628 (XXV, 1970), 2727 (XXV, 1970), and 2799 (XXVI, 1971).[27] According to noted international legal scholar Gerhard von Glahn,

> the coming into force of the United Nations Charter ended. . . . the legality of title to territory through conquest. The relevant provisions of the instrument [especially article 2, paragraph 4] make it abundantly clear that, from a legal point of view, the use or threat of force, in violation of the obligations assumed under the Charter, to obtain territory from another state is clearly prohibited to all members of the organization. . . .[28]

The Declaration on Principles of International Law Concerning Friendly Relations and Cooperation among States points out the relationship between Israeli occupation and the principle of the inadmissibility of the acquisition of territory by force. "The territory of a state shall not be the object of military occupation resulting from the use of force in contravention of the provisions of the Charter. The territory of a state shall not be the object of acquisition by another state resulting from the threat or use of force. No territorial acquisition resulting from the threat or use of force shall be recognized as legal."[29] The United Nations Charter itself makes an indirect reference to this principle in article 2, section 4. This principle was also important in the Kellogg-Briand Pact of 1928 and in the Atlantic Charter of 1941.[30]

Now that the principles of territorial integrity and the inadmissibility of the acquisition of territory by force have been set forth, it is important to discuss these principles in the context of whether or not Israel should have been required to withdraw from the occupied territories under international law. If this principle had been strictly applied, Israel would have been required to withdraw to the borders in effect before June 5, 1967. Such strict application of this principle was made in the 1956 Suez crisis, in which Israel, Great Britain, and France were forced by the United Nations to withdraw from the territory they had taken.[31] The consensus among most member states of the United Nations following the 1967 confrontation was that both principles required immediate Israeli withdrawal from all territories occupied after the Six-Day War.[32]

Israeli supporters first attempted to justify the continuing military occupation of Arab lands by citing the nonapplicability of principles of international law with regards to international relations. Nathaniel Lorch, a member of the Israeli delegation to the United Nations, summed up this position by saying, "we are still far away from a concept of international relations controlled or governed by the rule of law."[33] The importance of the use of international law in conflict resolution, Israel's persistent defiance of international law, and her enforcement of this defiance by "physical superiority" left her political legitimacy open to question. And it was this constant, unabated defiance of international law which left the Arabs no recourse but to fight.[34]

Israel and her supporters also saw withdrawal from the occupied territories as one step in an Arab plan to eliminate Israel altogether and to replace her with a Palestinian state. Although the Arab leaders would no doubt have been happy at such a turn of events, they were realists and as such might have been willing to acknowledge the existence of the state of Israel and to end the twenty-five-year state of belligerency in exchange for the return of the Arab lands captured during the 1967 war.[35]

Israel next based her justification of continued occupation upon a claim to title stronger than the Arab claim to the occupied lands, because the Israeli claim is based upon a "defensive action."[36] Here the reader must recall, first, the Israeli propaganda campaign to try to blame Egypt for the start of the 1967 war and, second, that when the world realized that Israel had conducted a preemptive strike against Egypt in 1967, Israel then attempted to justify a preemptive strike under modern international law, but failed. Even if the Arab title to the occupied lands had originally been based on invasion of those lands in 1947, some twenty years of de facto Arab control would bring into play the international legal principle of de facto control, which prevents the use of force to alter the situation, whether or not the initial occupation was lawful. This principle was formulated to prevent recurrent disputes over ancient boundaries.[37]

The Israelis next challenged the applicability of the concept of the inadmissibility of the acquisition of territory by force. They contended that if this high-sounding principle were to be applied equally, half the world would change hands.[38] However, Dr. John Lawrence Hargrove, director of studies for the American Society of International Law, saw a distinct change in modern international law from classical international law which would override this Israeli contention. Dr. Hargrove stated in hearings before the subcommittee on the Near East of the House Foreign Affairs Committee that

> the [United Nations] Charter as I interpret it is intended to rule out the classic situation in which one settles his dispute by taking over a piece of his neighbor's territory and then exacting a peace settlement. This was the point, put in almost those terms, which President Eisenhower made in urging Israeli withdrawal [from the Sinai peninsula] in 1957. I am not aware of any conditions in the present situation which alter the fundamental considerations and principles involved therein.[39]

Another argument used by Israeli supporters was that a rule by which the occupant must withdraw from occupied territories before peace terms are agreed upon would give rise to more aggression, by assuring every prospective aggressor that, if he fails, he will be entitled to restoration of any territory he has lost.[40] An analysis of this argument will show its invalidity. The very purpose of aggression is the acquisition of additional territory; it was to prevent just such aggression that the United States went to war in two world wars, in Korea, and in Vietnam.[41] Thus, if continued possession of the fruits of aggression are to be denied through the enforcement of a rule of international law, a country is much less likely to commit aggression, for it has nothing to gain while having much to lose in the way of men and war matériel.

Finally, the Israelis justified their continued occupation of Arab territories by pointing to the Allied occupation of Germany and Japan following World War II.[42] It is important to note that the United Nations Charter was meant to replace this sort of system, in which the victor (like Rome salting the ruins of Carthage) is free to take any measures of which he is capable in pursuit of the illusive certainty that the original injury will never in the future be repeated.[43]

One of the reasons for the problems of the Middle East was that the United Nations had abandoned this principle of the inadmissibility of the acquisition of territory by force when it partitioned Palestine by resolution on November 29, 1947. The abandonment of this principle in 1947 was justified by the situation in the Middle East having reached crisis proportions with Britain's resignation of her mandate.[44]

At the end of the 1956 Suez crisis, Israel had been in a position similar to that in 1973, i.e., she occupied Arab territories in the Gaza Strip and the Sinai peninsula. The 1956 Suez crisis is important because it is an example of the actual enforcement of the principle of the inadmissibility of the acquisition of territory by force. General Assembly Resolution 997 of November 2, 1956, required prompt withdrawal of all forces to the 1949 armistice lines.[45] In 1956, as in 1967, Israel refused, however, to pull out of the Gaza Strip and Sharm El-Sheikh on the Sinai peninsula without obtaining the recognition and the secure borders she had fought for.[46] Unlike what was to happen in 1967, however, Israel's demands in 1956 were held to be inadmissible by Secretary General Dag Hammarskjöld,[47] who said:

> The United Nations cannot condone a change in the *status juris* resulting from military actions contrary to the provisions of the Charter. The Organization must, therefore, maintain that the *status juris* existing prior to such military action be re-established by a withdrawal of troops and by the relinquishment or nullification of rights asserted in territories covered by the military action and depending on it.[48]

The United States and the Soviet Union shared this position that no compromise could be made with nor guarantee extended to Israel in advance of her total withdrawal, since to do otherwise would have been tantamount to condoning such a change in the *status juris* by military action in contradiction to the Charter.[49] In a memorandum to President Eisenhower, Secretary of State John Foster Dulles noted,

> With respect to the Gaza Strip—it is the view of the United States that the United Nations General Assembly has no authority to require of either Egypt or Israel a substantial modification of the Armistice Agreement, which, as noted, now gives Egypt the right and responsibility of occupation. Accordingly, we believe that Israel's withdrawal from Gaza should be prompt and unconditional. . . . [T]he United Nations has properly established an order of events and an order of urgency and . . . the first requirement is that forces of invasion and occupation should withdraw.[50]

Thus, in 1956, with the combined pressures of the United States and the Soviet Union, Israel was forced to relinquish the Gaza Strip and the Sinai peninsula and to go back to the 1949 armistice lines.[51]

As was mentioned in chapter four, above, the principle of state sovereignty required the United Nations Emergency Force to have the permission of the Egyptian government in order to operate on Egyptian soil. The modern concept of a state's sovereignty and territorial integrity forbids the entry of foreign forces, even if international in composition and character, into territory of that state without its voluntary approval, unless such forces are dispatched by the Security Council for those enforcement actions taken under Chapter VII of the United Nations Charter.[52]

On February 28, 1972, the United Nations Security Council passed Resolution 313, demanding that Israel cease its ground and air operations in southern Lebanon and withdraw its forces from Lebanese territory.[53] Israel had sent forces into southern Lebanon in an attack against Arab guerrilla positions. The United Nations actions precluded Israel from taking any additional territory from Lebanon. The Security Council had passed numerous other resolutions condemning Israeli actions against Lebanon and demanding withdrawal of Israeli troops from Lebanon, e.g., Resolution 262 (1968), 270 (1969), 279 (1970), and 280 (1970). The Security Council also passed Resolutions 248 (1968), 256 (1968), and 265 (1969) condemning Israel for attacks on Jordan.[54] These are modern applications by the Security Council of the principle of the inadmissibility of the acquisition of territory by war.

The most noted attempt by the United Nations to achieve peace in the Middle East (in addition to Security Council Resolution 242 of 1967), came on February 8, 1971, when Ambassador Gunnar Jarring submitted an aide-mémoire to both sides, requesting simultaneous prior commitments from each party on condition that the other party make its commitment. The commitments to be made would be subject to the eventual settlement of the entire Middle East problem, which would include a just settlement for the Palestinian refugees. For the moment, Jarring requested Israel to give a commitment to withdraw its forces to the former international boundary between Egypt and the British mandate of Palestine. For doing only this, Israel would receive a commitment from the United Nations for satisfactory arrangements to be made for (1) establishing demilitarized zones in the formerly occupied Arab territories; (2) practical security arrangements in the Sharm El-Sheikh area for guaranteeing freedom of navigation through the Straits of Tiran; and (3) freedom of navigation through the Suez Canal. From Egypt, Israel would receive a commitment to enter into a peace agreement covering (1) termination of all claims or status of belligerency; (2) respect for and acknowledgment of each other's sovereignty, territorial integrity, and political independency; (3) respect for and acknowledgment of each other's right to live in peace within secure and recognized boundaries; (4) responsibility to all within their power to ensure that acts of belligerency or hostility do not originate from within their respective territories against the population, citizens, or property of the other party; and (5) noninterference in each other's domestic affairs.

Egypt immediately accepted the proposal. Yet despite the fact that Jarring's proposal contained everything that Israel had been yearning for and fighting for, she turned down the proposal.[55] Perhaps the best reason for the Israeli rejection of Jarring's proposal can be found in the internal politics of Israel. A significant portion of Israeli public opinion, led by the right-wing Gahal political party, is avowedly expansionist and opposes any withdrawal from the occupied Arab territories.[56] This position is evident in a statement by Israeli Defense Minister Moshe Dayan, who said that if confronted with the choice between peace and Sharm El-Sheikh, he would choose the latter.[57]

Yakov Malik, Soviet Ambassador to the United Nations, speaking as president of the Security Council, said during the middle of one debate on the Middle East, "References to Article 51 of the Charter are well known, but that Article spoke of the right to self-defense, not of the right to violate international law and the Charter or to acquire territory by force."[58] Thus, Israel's major justification for continued occupation, her defensive position in the 1967 war, should no longer serve as sufficient justification. Even if Israel's posture in that was defensive, that alone would not justify continued occupation or annexation, since article 51 says nothing to justify such acquisition of territory.

United Nations resolutions are inseparable from the Charter

principles and objectives, and they likewise place binding obligations upon the members. General Assembly Resolution 2625 (XXV, 1970) says, in part, "The principles of the Charter which are embodied in this declaration institute basic principles of international law and consequently [the United Nations General Assembly] appeals to all states to be guided by these principles in their international conduct and to develop their mutual relations on the basis of the strict observance of these principles."[59] Hence, even if Security Council Resolution 242 is disregarded for the time being, the terms of General Assembly Resolution 2625 outlaws "military occupation resulting from the use of force in contravention to the provisions of the Charter," and we have shown in chapter 4 that the force used by the Israelis was in contravention of the Charter; therefore, continued Israeli occupation of Arab lands following the 1967 war could not be justified. The right of Israel to "secure and recognized boundaries" was tempered by the "inadmissibility of the acquisition of territory by war." Thus, both under the terms of Resolution 242 and of modern international law in general, Israel had no right to maintain her occupation of the Arab lands captured in 1967. Israeli withdrawal from those territories was therefore required if international law was to be controlling.

6

Israeli Occupation and International Law

The 1967 Six-Day War was devastating, conclusive, and short. It brought under Israel's control a territory nearly four times the size of her own in area. At the same time, ironically, the additional territories shortened her military boundaries and lifted the threat of direct Arab assault against most of her border settlements.[1] From Egypt, Israel captured the Sinai peninsula and the Gaza Strip; from Syria, she captured the Golan Heights; and from Jordan, she took East Jerusalem and the West Bank.[2]

The Sinai peninsula comprises 45,000 square miles, 95 percent of all of the territory Israel occupied as a result of the 1967 war. Most of it is unfit for human habitation—a baking desert and too high and mountainous to admit even the possibility of irrigation. Its basic value is military, since Sharm El-Sheikh, near its southern tip, controls the entrance to the Gulf of Aqaba, on which the port city of Eilat is located. Israeli control of this area prevents Egypt from forming a blockade as she did in 1967, closing off Israel's only trade route with the nations of Asia. Control of the Sinai peninsula also gives her a buffer zone as protection from Egyptian ground attack.

Control of the Golan Heights basically provides a military advantage as well as a safety advantage by removing from Syrian control an area which had been used to shell Israeli villages. Meanwhile, control of the Gaza Strip and the West Bank shorten the defensible frontiers.[3]

The basic sources of legal rights in areas under military occupation are found in the Hague Resolutions Respecting the Laws and Customs of War on Land of Hague Convention IV of 1907 and in Geneva Convention IV Relative to the Protection of Civilian Persons in Time of War.[4] It was to investigate Israeli violations of these provisions that the United Nations Human Rights Commission sent a six-man fact-finding team to the occupied territory.[5]

Article 46 of the Hague Convention deals with private rights, forbidding the confiscation of private property and requiring that the lives and property rights, as well as the religious practices of the persons in the area, be respected. Article 56 deals with the limitations put upon the occupying power with respect to public property. All public property, including that owned by municipalities, states, and institutions of religion, education, charities, arts, and sciences, is to be treated as private property. Thus, all seizure of, or destruction or willful damage done to, such things as churches, schools, public buildings, ornaments, or works of art or science is forbidden under this article.[6]

Among the signatories to the Geneva Convention were Israel, Egypt, Lebanon, Syria, and Jordan. This convention was expressly held to prevent the recurrence of crises of which the Jews in particular had been the victims.[7] Article 49 of the Geneva Convention is the one most pertinent to this study, and it says, "Individual as well as mass forceable transfers as well as deportation of protected persons from occupied territory to the territory of the occupying power or to that of any other country, occupied or not, are prohibited, regardless of their motive. The Occupying Power shall not deport or transfer parts of its own civilian population into the territory it occupies."[8]

Under Article 47, persons in the occupied territory "shall not be deprived, in any case or in any manner whatsoever, of the benefits of the [Geneva] Convention by any annexation by the [Occupying Power] of the whole or part of the occupied territory." Article 6 provides that the terms of the convention remain in effect as long as the territory remains occupied, despite the termination of military operations in a conflict.[9] It was

Israeli violations of this last provision in particular that caused the United Nations Human Rights Commission to condemn the Israeli government for its failure to comply with the provisions of the Geneva Convention.[10]

The military occupant is thus not entitled to treat the occupied territory as his own or its inhabitants as his own subjects. Furthermore, the military occupant can only confer rights as against himself and within his own limited period of de facto rule.[11] Finally, the occupying state is only an administrator and user of public buildings, immovable property, forests, and agricultural undertakings belonging to the hostile state and situated in the occupied country.[12]

These limitations affect military occupation by placing the actual, de facto ruling authority in the hands of the occupying power while making his rights temporary and incidental for the purposes of war. The legal, de jure sovereignty remains vested where it was before the territory was occupied, although obviously the legal sovereign is unable to exercise his ruling powers in the occupied country.[13]

Israeli actions in East Jerusalem are an example of Israeli acts in connection with the occupied Arab territories. On June 28, 1967, the Israeli government passed Administrative and Judicial Order Number 1, extending Israel's law, jurisdiction, and administration to East Jerusalem.[14] Although annexation in law did not occur until 1970, with the Israeli Supreme Court decision in *Rejuni and Others* v. *Military Court in Hebron,* 24 (20) Pikei Tin (Judgments) 419,[15] this order was the beginning of annexation in fact.

The first thing the Israeli government did once annexation had taken place was to banish the mayor of East Jerusalem from the city and the country for publicly opposing the Israeli annexation. The government next razed to the ground the homes of some two hundred Arab families who lived near the Wailing Wall, in order to create a plaza for more visitors and worshippers. The families were given only a few hours to evacuate their homes before the bulldozers moved in, and no compensation was offered for the loss of their homes. Adding insult to injury, when the bulldozing was complete, the Israeli army held a vast victory celebration on the land.[16]

One year later, an order was issued by the Israeli government expropriating additional vast areas of Arab land, for which no compensation was paid. In this expropriation, more than 6,000 Arabs were removed from the city and dispersed. In addition to the private property which was confiscated, the Israeli government also expropriated five Moslem mosques and four schools. The land taken was to be used for residential developments and would be given exclusively to Jews.[17] The new Jewish quarter of Parnot Eshkol was then created, and some 7,000 additional housing units were to be built on confiscated Arab lands over the next three years.[18]

Annexation of the holy city of Jerusalem also meant a decrease in business and profits from foreign tourists. Arab-owned and -operated hotels have received practically no business, and these and other Arab-owned and -operated businesses function at a distinct disadvantage under Israeli laws, which openly favor their Jewish competitors.[19]

Since the annexation of East Jerusalem was not prompted by Israel's desire for security, that action aroused worldwide opposition.[20] No nation gave official recognition to the move, and the United Nations General Assembly voted 99-0 to censure Israel for that act of annexation and declared any changes in the status of Jerusalem null and void.[21] Israeli actions in East Jerusalem also constituted flagrant violations of Article 46 of the Hague Convention of 1907, the London Charter of 1945, and Articles 47 and 49 of the Geneva Convention of 1949, as well as violating even the most elementary of human rights.[22]

The Six-Day War was hardly twenty-four hours old when Israeli leaders were assuring foreign diplomats that they had not gone to war to acquire territory. Before the week had ended, however, the Israelis were saying that they would never return to their old borders.[23] A joke appreciated by Israelis at one time goes something like this, "Certainly Israel wants peace: a piece of Syria, a piece of Jordan, a piece of Egypt. . . ."[24] At the end of the Six-Day War, Israel had intended to keep only East Jerusalem and the Golan Heights. As time went on, however, more and more of the territories were added to the "exclusion" list, such as the Gaza Strip and territories along the coast of Eilat Bay.[25] In an interview that appeared in the November 23, 1972, issue of the magazine *L'Europes,* Italian journalist Oriana Fallaci reported that Israeli Prime Minister Golda Meier had told her Israel would never return the Golan Heights to Syria, Jerusalem to Jordan, or the Gaza Strip to Egypt. Israel also demanded Sharm El-Sheikh and a strip of land along Eilat Bay to link it to Israel. In addition, Israel wanted certain strategic areas in the Sinai peninsula. In regard to the West Bank, Israel was adamant in her stance that the Jordan River must not be open for Arab troops to cross and that territorial modifications must be major ones, in which there would be as little Arab population as possible on Israel's new territory.[26]

Although military strategy outweighed other factors, Israeli economic policy toward the occupied territories also became increasingly significant. The importance of economic policy is obvious. The longer the use of oil from the Sinai, the more difficult it becomes to give up. The more integrated Israel's economy with the Gaza Strip and the West Bank, the more difficult it is to sever commercial, agricultural, and trade links. Israel has operated the oil fields in the Sinai peninsula ever since 1967, and Israeli scientists and engineers have surveyed the peninsula for additional mineral resources.[27]

Because of the shortage of manpower in Israel, the Israeli government, propelled by the economy, sought additional labor from the West Bank and the Gaza Strip. In 1967, 20,000 Arab laborers from those occupied territories found employment in Israel. By June 1970, the number had reached 30,000, showing that economic integration between Israel and the occupied territories had become a reality.[28]

In another effort to link the occupied territory of Gaza to Israel, the Israeli government invalidated the Egyptian pound as the medium of exchange and replaced it with the Israeli pound. Also in Gaza, the Israelis deliberately worsened the economic conditions in an effort to "encourage" emigration of the inhabitants.[29]

Given free reign, the Israeli economic policy toward the occupied territories would mean reduction of the economy of the occupied territories to a position of almost entire dependence upon the economy of Israel for a long time after any end to the occupation. In this regard, the special fact-finding committee sent to the Middle East by the United Nations Human Rights Commission warned that their examination indicated the Israeli occupation was causing undue interference in the economic life of the occupied territories. This situation, in the long run, might prove both irreversible and detrimental to the economic future of the occupied territories.[30]

The Six-Day War brought nearly one million Arabs under Israeli military administration in the occupied areas. Pending a settlement, Israel regarded itself as responsible for the welfare and security of the population in the area it occupied.[31] However, immediately after commencing their military occupation of the Arab territories captured during the war, the Israeli government enforced a policy aimed at the eviction of the largest possible number of Arab inhabitants from the towns and villages in the Gaza Strip, the West Bank of Jordan, and the Golan Heights, an eviction which, in many cases, was followed immediately by the settlement there of Jewish citizens of Israel.[32] While politicians were debating the fate of the occupied territories, the Arab people were steadily being driven from their homes and land in those territories, and new Jewish settlements were being founded in their place. This tendency to colonize more and more territory has been inseparable from the deepest economic and political dynamic of Israeli society and from its Zionist ideological basis.[33]

The tactics of Israeli military occupation were most severe in the Gaza Strip. Economic conditions, which were bad to start with in this area, were deliberately worsened in order to force the people in the area to leave. Since the members of the Israeli cabinet were resolved to annex the area eventually and since they also did not want to annex a large Arab population, this tactic seemed to them a logical course of action.[34] Thus, the area was subjected to a premeditated policy of depopulation and change of demographic structure and geographic composition. These policies, however, most certainly contravene the 1949 Geneva Convention, which strictly prohibits the establishment of settlements in occupied territories, the forcible deportation of the civilian population, and the destruction of houses and villages. The Geneva Convention also prohibits the changing of the geographic structure and demographic composition of occupied territories. Yet acts similar to those in the Gaza Strip were also committed by the Israeli government in the Egyptian Sinai peninsula, in the Syrian Golan Heights, and in the Jordanian sector of Jerusalem as well as on the West Bank.[35]

In the first days of the Six-Day War in 1967, Israeli forces took over three Arab border villages, Anivas, Yalu, and Bait Nuba, in the Latrun area without meeting any Arab opposition. The villages were then literally wiped off the map, as all houses and other buildings were demolished by bulldozers. The villagers were allowed to leave the area with only their lives, and their lands were distributed among neighboring Israeli farmers.[36] Over 3,000 acres were confiscated, while over 5,000 Arabs were rendered homeless, landless, and destitute.[37]

At about the same time, the Arab villagers of Zeita were assembled at six in the morning by the Israeli Army. They remained under armed guard all day under a blistering one-hundred-degree June sun, while other Israeli soldiers demolished the sixty-seven houses of the village, as well as the school and a clinic which had been run by the International Council of Churches. At six o'clock that evening, the Israeli commander appeared with a loudspeaker and told the villagers that they could return to their homes.[38]

Besides expelling Arabs still living in the territories occupied following the Six-Day War, Israel also prevented the return of thousands of inhabitants who, for one reason or another, had happened to be away from their homes on the West Bank or in the Gaza Strip when the Six-Day War began. The most effective device used to prevent the inhabitants from returning—and thereby permanently expelling them—was Order Number 125, issued by the commander of the Israeli defense forces on the West Bank. Under this order, any person who had been absent from the West Bank or any other occupied territory as of June 7, 1967, and who subsequently attempted to enter any of the occupied territories without an authorization issued solely by Israeli authorities, would be considered to be an infiltrator. Persons convicted of that offense were liable to punishments ranging from a minimum of fifteen years to a maximum of life imprisonment. The effectiveness of this measure in permanently expelling Arab inhabitants—who would, by the way, forfeit any lands or belongings to the Israeli military Government—is readily apparent. Of the over 170,000 applicants for reentry permits, only 14,027, or about eight percent, were issued permits and allowed to return. Israel, of course, lost no time in replacing the expelled Arabs with Jewish settlers. These groups of settlers, called *Nahal,* are young farmer-soldiers attached to the Israeli defense forces. Upon their arrival, they begin their duties by building their own homes.[39]

The effectiveness of the Israelis in expelling the Arab population from the occupied territories was even more evident in the Syrian Golan Heights. Before the 1967 war, there had been about 123,000 Syrians living in that area. By 1973, there were less than 5,000 persons—mainly of the Druze sect of the Muslim faith, who stayed in the area around Majd al-Shams. During that period Israel allowed only 83 persons to return to the area. At the same time, 15,000 Jewish settlers established military kibbutzim in the area, and plans were being made for the establishment of a city of 50,000 inhabitants.[40]

In all the occupied territories, the Israelis induced many Arab inhabitants to leave the area by various means of intimidation and collective punishment. One example of this method of inducement occurred at a refugee camp in the Gaza Strip. A small homemade bomb went off in the fish market. No one was hurt, and there was little damage. Yet, unable to apprehend the culprit, the Israeli army blew up several fishermen's storehouses and destroyed some of the fishing boats.[41]

In addition to the Israeli effort to physically drive the Arab population out, there is a second Israeli effort to change the character of the region, aimed principally at those people who have been "allowed" to remain. This policy—aimed at obliterating Arab culture, traditions, and customs—continued to be pursued in flagrant violation of the basic rights of the Arab people, as set forth in the United Nations Charter and in the Universal Declaration of Human Rights and as provided for in the Geneva Convention of 1949 and international law in general.[42]

The norm of conduct required of an occupying power should be reviewed at this point. That norm lies in international law and in particular in the Geneva Convention of 1949, to which Israel and the Arab countries are signatories. The Geneva Convention was intended to give "protected persons," that is, civilians under military occupation, certain fundamental rights which occupying powers were bound to observe. Article 53 prohibits the destruction of property; Article 33 prohibits collective punishment and the punishment of an individual who has not personally committed a crime; Article 49 prohibits, "regardless of motive," the transportation or deportation of any member of the population under military occupation from the occupied territory and also prohibits the occupying power from transferring its own population into the area it occupies; and Article 27 provides special protection for women.[43]

If the occupying power exceeds the limitations placed upon it by international law, the finger of censure is bound to be pointed in its direction. When the United Nations Human Rights Commission appointed its six-man fact-finding team in August 1969 to investigate charges of Israeli mistreatment of the Arab civilians in the occupied territories, the Israeli government rejected any cooperation with that committee and blocked its entry into numerous occupation zones. Nevertheless, the committee continued its investigations and obtained enough evidence to determine that numerous violations of the Geneva Convention did, in fact, exist, for which the United Nations Human Rights Commission condemned Israel.[44] A separate United Nations investigating committee, comprised of three nations and formed by the General Assembly in 1968, concluded in its 1972 report that Israel had displaced 11,000 Arabs in 1972 alone, particularly in the Gaza Strip and the Sinai peninsula, and had established forty-three settlements in the occupied territories since the 1967 war. The committee warned that Israel would make the occupied territories socially, economically, politically, and juridically part of Israel unless some form of supervision of the occupation was put into effect immediately to arrest such a trend.[45]

United Nations investigative bodies verified that Israel had violated the Geneva Convention and basic human rights by their acts of collective punishment, resort to harsh treatment, arbitrary detentions, destruction of Arab homes and other Arab properties, individual and mass deportations, and colonization and settlement of occupied lands. Thus, the following organizations condemned Israeli policies in the occupied territories: the Security Council (Resolution 271 in 1969), the General Assembly (Resolutions 2535 B–XXIV, December 10, 1969; 2546–XXIV, December 11, 1969; and 2727–XXV, December 15, 1970); the Commission on Human Rights (Resolutions 6–XXV, March 4, 1969; 10–XXVI, March 23, 1970; and 9–XXVII, March 15, 1971); the International Conference on Human Rights held in Tehran (Resolution 1, May 7, 1968); the World Health Assembly of the World Health Organization (Resolutions 23.52, May 21, 1970, and 24.33, May 18, 1971); and the Executive Board of UNESCO (Resolutions 83 EX / 4.4.2, April / May 1969, and 83 EX / 4, September / October 1969).[46]

In essence, the reports of the Red Cross and the United Nations committees of investigation and the statements issued by many international humanitarian organizations all attest that the situation in the areas under Israeli military occupation was intolerable. Consequently, the measures undertaken by Israel in the occupied territories have been considered war crimes and an affront to humanity. However, the foreign minister of Israel defended these policies, asserting that Israel, indeed, applied humanitarian principles in the areas of its occupation. According to him, Israel increased the number of television sets in the hands of the people under its occupation.[47]

The fact that more people in the occupied territories had television sets, however, in no way offsets the fact that thousands of Arab inhabitants were subject to outright eviction from their homes and lands, while countless others faced indirect intimidation and were forced to flee their land. All these methods, direct and indirect, made up a scheme which seems to serve a single overriding purpose: the gradual de-Arabization of the occupied territories and the concurrent establishment there of Jewish settlements which could eventually be utilized to stake a claim in the occupied territory in the tradition of the fait accompli which was efficiently used by the Zionist movement in Palestine before 1948 and which paved the way for the establishment of the state of Israel in that year.[48]

The state of Israel was a product of a colonization movement, and it remains an instrument of continuing colonization. This fact is attested to by the confiscation of lands in East Jerusalem, in the Golan Heights, and in Hebron, and other West Bank areas to build Jewish settlements. It is also evidenced by the very words of Israeli leaders. Moshe Dayan, Israeli defense minister, told a group of American Jewish students in the Golan Heights just a year after the 1967 Six-Day War that, "During the last hundred years, our people have been in the process of building up the nation, of expansion, of getting additional Jews and settlements in order to expand the borders. Let no Jew say that the process has ended. Let no Jew say we are near the end of the road."[49] Thus, the Israelis remained on a continuing road toward further expansion. This road can be traced to Zionist ideology which can no longer be described as an irrelevant anachronism.[50]

Zionist ideology with respect to the Israeli settlement of the conquered Arab territories is clearly evident. The Twenty-seventh Zionist Congress in Jerusalem observed, "The crucial question confronting us is how we are to populate with Jews the newly liberated areas, at a time when Jews, living in countries from which egress is possible, are unwilling to come and settle here."[51] The conclusion is obvious that the Zionist movement was definitely concerned with populating the occupied Arab territories with Jews as the Israeli Army continued to depopulate the areas of many of their Arab inhabitants.

Moshe Dayan pointed out three reasons for establishing settlements in the occupied territories. The first, a political and security reason, asserted that settlements were necessary in the areas from which the Israeli government did not intend to withdraw. Thus, the digging of wells and the cultivating of land became a necessity in those areas. The second reason comes from the historical point of view. Certain settlements, such as Hebron, were established because the people of Israel consider themselves attached to the area by the links of a people with its heritage and homeland. The third criterion was an economic one. Establishment at settlements cannot be separated from economic considerations, and hence new centers of settlement should be established near army camps.[52]

In general, the Israelis proceeded to establish scores of settlements in the occupied territories, and by 1973 plans were underway for the establishment of additional settlements, including a city for 250,000 Jewish inhabitants in the southern part of the Gaza Strip. At Sharm El-Sheikh, for example, Israel lay claim to the area and established a number of settlements. It also built a road to connect Sharm El-Sheikh to Israel and then planned to annex a large strip of the Sinai peninsula to insure that connection.[53]

Between the 1967 war and the 1973 war, the Israeli government established fifteen settlements in the Syrian Golan Heights, another fifteen settlements on the Jordanian West Bank, and fourteen additional settlements in the formerly Egyptian areas of the Gaza Strip and the Sinai peninsula.[54] The Israeli government spent 280,000,000 Israeli pounds in building these new settlements.[55] There were divergent reports as to the number of Israeli settlers there. The government claimed that only 4200 Israelis settled in the occupied territories following 1967, including the *Nahal* military settlements.[56] A private source, however, listed the number as 15,000 such settlers.[57]

The Israeli government claimed in 1967 that the settlements, such as the one in Hebron, were carried out independently of the government and that the areas had not been annexed. It must be remembered, however, that during the war three ancient Arab villages in the Latroun area along the Israeli-Jordanian border had been destroyed, their population of five thousand Arabs had been dispersed, and over three thousand acres of land had been given to Israeli farmers. Moreover, the Eshkol government had sanctioned a small number of *Nahal* settlements, the setting up of which began in August 1970.[58] A few months later, *Nahal* settlements were started in the Syrian Golan Heights, and shortly after that, other *Nahal* settlements were begun in the Jordan Valley. In all, during the first year of occupation alone, the Israeli government spent 18,000,000 Israeli pounds in establishing eighteen settlements in the occupied territories, including ten settlements in the Syrian Golan Heights, three settlements on the Jordanian West Bank, and five in the Egyptian Negev and Sinai peninsula.[59] These settlements were but a part of Israel's master plan for settlements in the occupied territories.[60]

Israel Galili, chairman of the Ministerial Committee for the Settlement of the Occupied Territories and minister without portfolio, told the Israeli Knesset on July 17, 1972, that no area was out of bounds to Jewish settlement and that, "the settlement policy is not dictated by security, but by historical right as well—if not more so."[61] Maps on display in Tel Aviv bookshops did not list the West Bank by that name or as belonging to Jordan, but as the Israeli "provinces" of Jordan and Samaria.[62] At the same time, Tiran had been renamed Yotvat, Sharm El-Sheikh was called Mifratz Shlome, the Gulf of Aqaba was renamed the Gulf of King Soloman, and the Golan Heights became the Hogolan.[63]

The whole point to the discussion of Israeli settlement in the occupied territories is that those settlements were intended to be permanent, with the land becoming a part of Israel. This goal can be seen in the actions of Israeli leaders as they (1) referred to a "greater Israel"; (2) claimed that Jordan and Egypt had no legal claim to the West Bank and the Gaza Strip areas and that Syria could not be permitted to regain control of the Golan Heights because of the danger to Israeli villages; (3) pressed for large-scale Jewish immigration, especially from the West, so that Israel's bargaining position over the disposition of the occupied lands would be improved with a large Jewish population needing land for new settlement; and (4] kept the population balance of Jews to Arabs at a constant two-to-one ratio in favor of the Jews. The last of these is the most difficult, since the Arabs have a much higher birthrate.[64] The issue of settlement has also been distinguished from the issue of security, as Moshe Dayan noted when he said, "A distinction must be made between the occupation of places purely from the security point of view and of places where settlement must be taken into consideration. If it was purely a security problem we could station tank divisions and Nahal paratroopers; there would be no need to plant tomatoes."[65] Thus, the ultimate purpose of Israeli settlements, economic integration with the occupied territories, and the human ties was to create a new portion of land for the Jewish state.[66]

The establishment of Israeli settlements in occupied Arab territories had no legal basis other than force and conquest.[67] It remained a continuing violation of both the Geneva Convention of 1949 and the Hague Convention of 1907, and of the London Charter of 1945. It violated a basic principle of modern international law: the inadmissibility of the acquisition of territory by force. Hence, Israel's military supremacy could create no rights, for none had previously existed.

7

Israel's Security and the Question of Borders

Prior to the Six-Day War of 1967, Israel had never complained about her security and the vulnerability of the armistice lines. Quite the contrary, before June 5, 1967, Israel had considered her boundaries to be highly satisfactory, and her main goal for eighteen years had been to make those lines into permanent and recognized frontiers. As Foreign Minister Abba Eban told the United Nations General Assembly in October 1966,

> Behind the armistice frontiers established by agreement between Israel and its Arab neighbors in 1949, the national life of sovereign states has become crystallized in an increasingly stable mold. There is some evidence that thoughtful minds in the Middle East are becoming skeptical about threats to change the existing territorial and political structure by armed force. Such threats and policies concerted to support them offend the spirit and letter of the United Nations Charter. They violate bilateral agreements freely negotiated and solemnly signed. . . . [W]e regard the present armistice lines as immune from any change without consent.[1]

Following the 1967 conflict, however, the Israelis were adamant in their demand for "secure and recognized boundaries." Israel has defended all of her actions after 1967 with the argument that those measures were necessary to insure her security. In order for peace to come about in the Middle East, as President Johnson observed in a speech on September 10, 1968, "Arab governments must convince Israel and the world community that they have abandoned the idea of destroying Israel. But equally, Israel must persuade its Arab neighbors and the world community that Israel has no expansionist designs on their territory."[2] Thus, it becomes important to determine, first, what Israel's demands were in the way of security, and second, if she went beyond her security requirements and into expansion of her territory.

The overriding demand of Israel is for security. The Arabs find this hard to accept, since their knowledge of Zionism is primarily based on their firsthand experience of being invaded, overrun, and bombed—of having their own security destroyed. However, no one who has visited Israel and talked to the Israelis can doubt that the overwhelming majority would be willing to make considerable concessions if they believed that this would increase their security.[3] The question remains, though, What concessions would the Israeli government be willing to make to increase Israel's security?

Israel defines secure borders as those borders which by their very nature reduce the danger and threat of war and consequently increase the chances for a lasting peace.[4] In its justification of "allowing Israel to acquire additional territory," the United States called the additional territory and new borders "buffer zones," which the U.S. stated Israel needed to "protect" herself from her neighbors. Yet Israel's speedy defeat of all her neighbors combined caused no one to wonder just who really needed protection.[5]

Israel bases her demand for secure borders on the sanctity of human life and the right of Israel to exist as a state. Her purpose is to try to free future generations of Israelis from the necessity of fighting endless wars for the survival of the state.[6] If any future fighting is necessary, the Israelis would rather it be done in the occupied territories than in Israel proper.[7] Thus, the Israelis may very well argue that the 1973 confrontation indicated the need to retain the 1967 conquests to maintain Israel's security.

Israel has maintained that the only way to determine these

borders is through direct negotiations with the Arabs.[8] Direct negotiations between the parties are particularly necessary because border changes are involved.[9] In the face of the Israeli intention to keep all or most of the occupied territories, however, the Arabs feel they have no choice but to refuse to negotiate—for they have little to negotiate with, while at the same time they would lose their present rights as belligerents.[10]

Most of the occupied territories do seem to have had a relation to Israel security needs. Israel claimed that the Golan Heights and the Gaza Strip had been repeatedly used for launching attacks on her and asserted that the Sinai peninsula and the West Bank have an important strategic location in relation to her overall security needs.[11] The new borders which Israel gained with retention of the territories occupied in 1967 gave her every strategic advantage her military leaders ever sought. The Gaza Strip was eliminated as a military threat to central Israel, while the military frontier with Egypt was shortened by several hundred kilometers.[12] Moreover, Israeli control of Sharm El-Sheikh at the southern tip of the Sinai peninsula virtually assured Israel's control of the Gulf of Aqaba, where the Israeli port of Eilat is situated. Israeli trade with Asian nations must go through the Gulf of Aqaba. Control of the Golan Heights was also primarily of military importance, for it was from this area that the Syrians used to rain bullets and shells on Israeli villages below.[13] Hence, the new Israeli security line was far removed from the heart of Israel.[14]

Israel contended that she had never had state boundaries until after the Six-Day War, and considered the boundaries of before June 5, 1967, to be merely provisional military lines.[15] Israel also asserted that since the beginning of her existence in 1948, the Arab states have considered themselves in a state of war with her and that because of this, no Arab-Israeli boundary can be considered permanent.[16]

It must be remembered that as late as October 1966, Israel had assented to the June 5, 1967, boundaries established before and desired their permanence—their being "immune from any change without consent." Consent must be interpreted as meaning the consent of both the Arabs and the Israelis, for any other interpretation would "offend the spirit and the letter of the United Nations Charter." Moreover, when the international community of nations separately recognized the existence of the state of Israel, that recognition was based on the boundaries defined in the United Nations partition plan. In other words, all allocation of territory to Israel was done in the United Nations resolution. Therefore, the question becomes, Will the international community sanction Israel's acquisition of additional territory by force? Certainly neither the General Assembly nor the Security Council of the United Nations could partition Egypt, Jordan, and Syria and give sections to Israel.[17] Hence, the United Nations should not allow Israel to achieve the same result by resorting to the use of force. Going one step further, Chaidir Anwar Sani, representative to the United Nations from the Republic of Indonesia, said to the Security Council,

> Indonesia appreciates the need for secure and recognized boundaries. That cannot be interpreted to mean they should be imposed by military means or that they should be the result of a change by force of internationally recognized frontiers. That would be clearly against the principle of the inadmissibility of the acquisition of territory by war and of respect of territorial integrity and the inviolability of international frontiers.[18]

The border between the Egyptian Gaza Strip and Israel before June 5, 1967, is an example of an internationally recognized frontier[19] which cannot be changed by force without violating the above-named principles of international law.

In addition, the fact that for nearly twenty years de facto control of the occupied territories rested with the Arab countries might in itself give rise to Arab rights to the land.[20] Moreover, for nearly twenty years the international community treated the 1949 armistice lines as definitive of the rights of both sides under Article 4, Section 2, of the United Nations Charter, even though the boundaries in and of themselves were not regarded as permanent. Therefore, for the international community to reward the exercise of force by altering their position would seriously injure the principle of peaceful settlement of disputes and the non-use of force against the territory of another.[21] Even the United States, a staunch supporter of Israel, sees the 1949 armistice lines as definitive of the obligations of the parties under the United Nations Charter respecting the nonuse of force against each other.[22]

The Israelis have found themselves faced with a dilemma caused by the conflict between their actions to maximize their security and their statements of justification. Both Israeli statements and actions in regard to their security were based on the premise that the Arab states are committed to Israel's destruction. The wide acceptance and the constant reinforcement of this premise by the Israelis have made it extremely difficult for them to attain the feeling of being secure. As a result, Israel has concentrated her efforts on maximizing the objective conditions of security, such as the preservation of her military superiority, on extending her frontiers to more defensible positions, and on tightening her control within the occupied Arab territories. But as Charles Yost, former United States ambassador to the United Nations, has pointed out, it is a myth to believe that strategic boundaries and military strength can provide Israel more permanent security than could an agreed settlement and international guarantees.[23]

Israel's premise that the Arabs were committed to her destruction was itself false. Although Arab leaders would no doubt have been happy at Israel's demise, they were realists and had in practice recognized Israel's existence.[24] Yet, Israel saw her withdrawal from the occupied territories as the first part of an Arab program leading to her ultimate destruction and her replacement by a Palestinian state.[25] Though Israel's only chance of long-term security required that she withdraw to the frontiers in effect before June 5, 1967, her deeply felt fears and suspicions inhibited her from seizing that chance. Retention of the occupied territories made Israel's demand to be allowed to live in peace—though sincere—sound increasingly hollow, like the plea of a burglar to be left alone with his loot.[26]

Thus, it is a sad feature of human behavior that insecurity

breeds aggressiveness. Because of the treatment they have received throughout history, the Jewish people are haunted by an almost pathological sense of insecurity. This leads them to seek power over their opponents in ways which, by tragic paradox, create the very dangers that they are so anxious to avoid.[27] In the words of Arnold Wolfers, a noted international observer, "The quest for security points beyond mere maintenance and defense. It can be so ambitious as to transform itself into a goal of unlimited self-extension."[28] This transformation can be readily seen in the Israeli quest for security, for—as in the past—Israel stressed her demand for security, implying the need for more territory. This linking of territorial expansion with the problem of security is an equation central to Zionist political ideology and is exemplified by the refusal of the Israeli government to accept peace without the enlargement of its territory through retention of most, if not all, of the occupied territories.[29]

Although Israel claimed to recognize the Arab nations' right to secure borders,[30] her obsession with the physical and circumstantial factors of her own security made a mockery of the concept of territorial integrity for the neighboring Arab states. It induced Israel to rob her Arab neighbors of any and all semblance of security. For Israel to enjoy the feeling of being secure, her Arab neighbors would have had to accept a position of insecurity and the violation of their territorial integrity. Since these terms were unacceptable to them, Israel continued to perceive the Arab states as a threat to her security,[31] despite the fact that the Israeli army were occupying Arab lands and that Israeli troops and air force attacked Arab countries whenever and wherever they chose.[32] This is exemplified by numerous excursions by the Israeli army into southern Lebanon and by the Israeli air strikes against an Egyptian scrap metal factory on February 12, 1970, in which seventy persons were killed and hundreds of others injured.[33]

Yet, American news reporters and commentators continued to report that the Arabs threatened Israel and were intent upon her destruction. Whenever Israel struck at her Arab neighbors (as in the examples above), however, such actions were defended, and Israeli arguments were repeated as proof of the logic and rightness of the Israeli acts.[34]

Israel relied on military power by perpetuating a state of superiority in armaments and, because of her insecurity, relied on the idea of dominating her neighbors. The Israelis acted on the assumption that the best chance of safety was to dominate their Arab neighbors militarily, including the seizing and holding of tactically advantageous territory far beyond their own frontiers.[35] Security to the Israelis also meant insuring that the Arabs would never be able to regain any territory that Israel might decide it needs. Hence, with its superiority in armaments and its control of the occupied territories, Israel has had the opportunity to effect all the changes it wished to bring about.[36] Yet no country occupying tens of thousands of square miles of its neighbors' territory and ruling over more than a million of their people with an increasingly heavy hand can expect to live in peace—or, indeed, deserves to do so.[37]

Israel's aggressive policy toward her Arab neighbors was not due solely to her pathological feelings of insecurity. The fact that the state of Israel originated in a movement of colonization and that she knows that in the eyes of her Arab neighbors she was a usurper of conquered lands makes her relationship with them one based solely on force. In Israel's view, her adversaries should have only one position from which to bargain—that of the conquered.[38] Thus, Israel continued her policies of faits accomplis in the occupied territories, which demanded the complete capitulation of an enemy who refuses to submit.[39] The fact remains that Israeli policy was predicated on the belief that the all-consuming passion of her Arab neighbors was to destroy her and that only the realization of her invincibility prevented them from doing so.[40] However, colonization seems to have been an equally important factor in Israeli policy, as Defense Minister Moshe Dayan noted in saying, "A distinction must be made between the occupation of places purely from the security point of view and of places where settlement must be taken into consideration as well as security. If it was purely a security problem we could station tank divisions . . . ; there would be no need to plant tomatoes."[41] An example of Israeli policy where security considerations played no role whatsoever was in Israel's annexation of Jordanian East Jerusalem.[42]

As was earlier noted, Israeli minister Israel Galili told the Israeli Knesset in July 1972 that no area was out of bounds to Jewish settlements. Since Israeli settlements were shown in the last chapter to be intended to lead to ultimate annexation, it can be concluded that Israel's territorial ambitions were also dictated more by historical considerations than by security needs.[43] As Defense Minister Moshe Dayan told the youth of the United Labor party after the 1967 war, "Our fathers made the borders of 1947. We made the borders of 1949. You made the borders of 1967. Another generation will take the frontiers to where they belong."[44]

Israel's belief that control over vast Arab territories would improve her security situation has proven sadly mistaken. Israel's vast military victory in 1967 did not put an end to guerrilla and sabotage activity by Palestinian guerrillas,[45] as evidenced by incursions into Lebanon. This disproved the Zionist belief that the Palestinian commandos had no will of their own and that resistance would wither away once Egypt had been forced to submit.[46] It therefore seems that Israel's only chance for a lasting peace lies in withdrawal from the occupied territories.

Israel defends her right to secure and recognized boundaries under United Nations Security Council Resolution 242 of November 22, 1967. However, the resolution provides that "every state in the area"—not just Israel—has the right to live in peace within secure and recognized boundaries. Hence, the resolution calls for and provides for Arab security as well as Israeli, and Israeli security cannot be purchased at the expense of Arab security. Moreover, Resolution 242 also emphasizes the United Nations Charter principles of the "inadmissibility of the acquisition of territory by force" and the "territorial integrity of states." Thus, a state is deprived of its territorial integrity whenever any part of its territory is forcibly separated for whatever reason. Annexation of territory acquired by means of war is, in addition, clearly prohibited by modern international law.[47] As has been shown, interpretation of Security Council Resolution 242 doesn't entail only the Israeli requirement of secure and recognized boundaries.

In essence, the concept of secure and recognized boundaries in no way contradicts the principle of Israel's withdrawal from the occupied territories.[48] Security of boundaries does not mean annexation of more boundaries, but comes through a peaceful settlement which is not detrimental to either side. Such an idea was put forth by William Rogers when he was United States secretary of state. He stated that "[Any territorial changes] should not reflect the weight of conquest and should be confined to insubstantial alterations, . . . [for] the acquisition of territory is no guarantee of security."[49]

8

A Critical Look at Israeli Arguments

The purpose of this chapter is just what the title indicates. In the course of their defenses of the many actions they have taken with regard to the occupied territories, the Israelis and their supporters have put forth a number of arguments, many of which have been accepted as fact without their being analyzed or any attempt being made to refute them. In the Arab-Israeli confrontation—just as in a debate, a trial, or a general dispute—there were valid issues and arguments on both sides. As has been stressed throughout this volume however, it was usually the Israeli position which received the more sympathetic attention in analyses of the Middle East confrontation. This is basically because the Israelis had a most favorable image in the press, particularly in the American press, where many facts and arguments were not presented for discussion. Therefore, a fresh look at the arguments put forth by both sides is needed to determine the validity of each position. The major issues in the Arab-Israeli confrontation—i.e., who started the 1967 war, the control of the media, the question of Israeli withdrawal, the question of Israeli treatment of the Arab inhabitants, the question of Israeli settlements, and the question of secure borders—have been discussed already in earlier chapters. This chapter will try to focus on those arguments which may never have appeared in the headlines, but which are important nonetheless in analyzing the Arab-Israeli dispute.

The first Israeli argument to be dealt with is the one that international law is not applicable to Israeli conduct in the Arab-

Israeli confrontation. This argument evolved from a statement by Nathaniel Lorch, member of the Israeli delegation to the United Nations, implying that present international relations were neither controlled nor governed by the rule of law. Irving M. Engle, former president of the American Jewish Committee, went even further, saying that at most, law has played only a small role in the Arab-Israeli conflict.[1] This attitude by the Israelis toward the role of international law in the Middle East conflict was even noted by Egyptian Foreign Minister Mohammed H. El-Zayyat, who said,

> That [the Israeli acts in the occupied territories are] incompatible with the United Nations Charter must be irrelevant to the Israelis. The United Nations has no guns; the United Nations has no jets. Israel does not need the United Nations now and does not want it to interfere. Israel wants to finish its unfinished business with the Arabs outside the Organization, outside the Charter, outside the law.[2]

However, the importance of international law and its connection with international relations was found to be very important indeed by the late President Dwight D. Eisenhower, who said in a speech on October 31, 1956, "There can be no peace—without law. And there can be no law—if we were to invoke one code of international conduct for those who oppose us and another for our friends."[3] Thus, the importance of international law is in its ability to maintain international peace. The primary organ for keeping this peace has been the United Nations. Their purpose is to settle disputes, or at least to attempt to settle them, and to take measures for the prevention and removal of threats to peace. Members of the United Nations are obligated to obey international laws contained in the Charter and resolutions of the United Nations[4] in order to maintain the world peace which is so important in today's nuclear age.

Israel's next argument was that the commitment of neighboring Arab countries to her destruction caused them under international law to forfeit any claims they might have had to the occupied Arab territories. Speaking before the Security

Council, Israeli Representative Yosef Tekoah said, "Surrounded by states which refused to recognize the justice of the Jewish people's rebirth in its historic homeland and which aspired to Israel's destruction, Israel would be fully entitled, morally and legally, to conclude that the Arab states have forfeited all their claims in relation to Israel."[5] This argument was again based on the faulty premise that the Arab states were bent on the elimination of the state of Israel at all costs, whereas, in fact, the Arab states recognized the existence of Israel in practice, though not diplomatically.[6] Moreover, as pointed out in earlier chapters, the argument that Israel was in danger of extinction in 1967 was later admitted by the members of the Israeli cabinet to have been a figment produced by their fertile minds to justify the annexation of the occupied Arab territories.[7] In addition, this Israeli argument involves a misapplication of international law by asserting that the Arab countries had forfeited their interest in the lands occupied by Israel in 1967 because they desired Israel's ultimate destruction.

This assertion of forfeiture is directly contrary to the fundamental principle of the territorial sovereignty of each state upon which the United Nations Charter is based. Hence, the acquisition of territory can come about only by the cession by a former sovereign to the new sovereign.[8] Moreover, Israel could not claim the forfeiture of anyone's right to the occupied territories, since she had no right to be there herself. Even if in 1967 she lawfully went to war under Article 51 of the United Nations Charter, her right to remain in those territories ended once she had crushed the Arab opposition which had caused the "danger" to her security.[9] As has been discussed, however, Israel could not in fact justify her actions as being in self-defense, and therefore she had no right to be in the occupied territories to begin with. Moreover, if Israel had not been occupying territories and if the Arab states desired her destruction, the Israeli argument would most certainly fall, for the United Nations could not partition Egypt, Jordan, and Syria and give sections to Israel.[10] Thus, the United Nations should not allow Israel to acquire territory under the Israeli rationale of Arab forfeiture of interest, for that would, in effect, be sanctioning the acquisition of that territory by force, in contradiction to one of the major principles of the United Nations Charter.

In chapter 5, the Israeli assertion of having a stronger claim to title than the Arab countries was discussed. Because of the importance of that argument, however, a second look at it is warranted. The argument, as presented by Associated Press reporter Myron S. Kaufmann, goes like this: "it should be pointed out that the Israeli occupation was entirely lawful according to international law. The Egyptian title to Gaza and the Jordanian title to the West Bank and to Jerusalem were bad, resting on unlawful invasion [in 1948]. . . . The Israeli title founded upon defensive action is better."[11] This argument rests entirely upon two inherently false assumptions: (1) that the Israeli action in 1967 was defensive, and (2) that an occupying power can assert legal sovereignty in occupied territories.

In analyzing the first assumption, it is important to remember that in 1967 it was Israel who conducted a preemptive strike—which literally means to attack them before they attack you. Israel is the *only* member of the international community to believe that a preemptive strike is a legitimate means of self-defense under Article 51 of the United Nations Charter,[12] which allows a member state to use armed force when it is under attack. Hence, all other nations see a preemptive strike as another form of aggression. Also, the United Nations Charter was intended to repudiate the legitimacy of the preemptive strike as a means of settling international disputes.[13] Therefore, the Israeli action was not based upon a defensive action, and under Kaufmann's own analysis, it could not give the Israelis a better claim to title than the Arabs had. The idea of Arab de facto control and its rights has been discussed already in chapter 5.

Looking to the second major assumption, that an occupying power can assert lawful sovereignty, it is important to look at the analysis of Israeli supporter Allen Gerson, who wrote: "The occupying power may not, however, lawfully assert sovereignty unless it can make a credible claim that the area constitutes a *res nullius* and as such is open to the first lawful entrant to exercise effective occupation, or that it possesses a latent right of sovereignty which is now superior *erga omnes*."[14] Thus, in order for an occupying power to assert legal sovereignty over the occupied territories, it must first show that there was no lawful sovereign in the area before the occupation; but it must also show that it is the first *lawful* entrant "to exercise effective occupation." Therefore, the fact that Israel is an unlawful entrant into the occupied territories precludes it from asserting any lawful sovereignty over the occupied territories.

If the occupying power fails to prove a *res nullius* and to establish that it is the first lawful entrant to occupy the area, it can still assert sovereignty if it can show "that it possesses a latent right of sovereignty which is now superior *erga omnes*": in other words, a historical right. This Israel has also asserted, which leads to their next argument: Jewish historical rights to occupied territories of the Gaza Strip, the Sinai Peninsula, and the West Bank. In 1956, Israeli Prime Minister David Ben-Gurion referred to the Sinai peninsula as being, not a part of Egypt proper, but part of the ancient Jewish homeland. In October 1969, Israeli Defense Minister Moshe Dayan spoke of the Israeli right to be in the West Bank.[15] And, as mentioned above, Israeli minister-without-portfolio Israel Galili said in July 1972 that Israel had the historical right to settle in the occupied territories,[16] settlements which were to become part of the state of Israel.

However, under modern international law as decided by the International Court of Justice in the 1962 Temple of Vihear case, arguments of a physical, historical, religious, and archeological character are not regarded as legally decisive as to the legal rights of parties.[17] Thus, it must be said that historical rights alone are not sufficient to give an occupying power, in this case Israel, the right to legally assert sovereignty over occupied territories.[18]

Following the 1967 war, Israel refused to comply with United Nations requests and resolutions demanding withdrawal from the occupied territories and called instead for direct negotiations between the parties to the conflict. Secretary-General U

Thant, in reporting the progress of UN Ambassador Gunnar Jarring to the General Assembly, said, "The Israeli Government has firmly adhered to the view that a settlement can be reached only through direct negotiations culminating in a peace treaty."[19] The Arabs saw the Israeli demand as an invitation to the "conquered countries" to meet their conqueror and to discuss the size of the fruits of conquest.[20] The Arabs based their stance on the fear that recognition or negotiation before withdrawal would enable Israel to gain legal status in the occupied territories prior to withdrawal.[21]

A further Israeli argument contended that her occupation of the Arab territories captured in the 1967 war had brought greater technical progress and a higher standard of living to the area. This argument was merely a revival of the nineteenth-century "white man's burden" argument used by colonial powers to justify their colonial expansion and was no real justification for Israeli occupation and annexation of Arab territories taken in the 1967 war.[22]

Israel claimed that because both the United Nations and the United States had failed to prevent Egyptian President Nasser from closing the Suez Canal and the Straits of Tiran and from massing Egyptian troops along the Egyptian-Israel border, Israel could not depend upon any future United Nations guarantees.[23] Another look at the Egyptian reasons behind their actions, the surrounding circumstances, and the United Nations in general will dispel this claim.

As discussed in chapter 4, it was not until May 1967 that Egyptian President Nasser committed the acts which Israel then used to justify their preemptive strike against Egypt. Those acts were committed in response to Israeli attacks upon Syria and to the threat of future attacks. Moreover, if the Israelis had feared for the life of their state, they could have allowed the United Nations Emergency Force to cross the Egyptian border into Israel. The Israelis, however, refused to allow the UNEF to enter Israel, thereby disproving the assertion that the United Nations had let Israel down in 1967. Furthermore, Chapter 7, Article 39, of the United Nations Charter permits the Security

Council to take whatever action it may deem necessary to stop any act of aggression, as it did in regard to Korea in 1950.

Israel also asserted that whether or not her attack upon Egypt was justifiable under international law, Israel had informed Jordan that she would not attack her unless Jordan initiated hostilities. While Jordan does not deny initiating such hostilities, she claims it was in response, as an ally of Egypt, to the attack upon Egypt by Israel and that it was justifiable under Article 51 of the United Nations Charter as a collective self-defense measure against an armed attack.[24]

The last issue to be examined in this chapter is that posed at the end of chapter 3 in connection with the argument by Professor Julius Stone concerning whether the rights of sovereignty over occupied lands can be restored to an illegal invader if the international community treats the illegal acquisition as legal.[25] As discussed in chapter 4, Israel's preemptive strike against Egypt on June 5, 1967, cannot be justified under Article 51 of the United Nations Charter as a self-defense measure and therefore her status in the occupied territories was that of an illegal invader-occupant with very few rights, and with no right to legal sovereignty in the occupied territories. She also did not have the approval of the international community which would have restored her those rights. This is evidenced by the December 13, 1971, General Assembly resolution calling for Israel to withdraw from all occupied Arab territories.[26]

9

The Arab Perception of the Middle East Crisis

In chapter 2, the point was discussed that the saturation of the news media with the pro-Israeli point of view made the Arab perspective sound unconvincing when it was presented. Now that the Israeli stance has been dissected and examined, a second look at the overall Arab point of view and its perception of the Arab-Israeli crisis is in order. The purpose of this chapter is to present a general overview of the Arab point of view now that the pro-Israeli bias has been dispelled.

Although Arab leaders are anti-Zionist and would no doubt have been happy to see the state of Israel dismantled, they were realistic enough not to make the destruction of Israel their objective. After 1967 they publicly supported and consistently worked for the implementation of United Nations Security Council Resolution 242.[1] Moreover, as mentioned above, since 1948 they have recognized Israel's existence in practice, though not granting her diplomatic recognition.

Dr. Kamel S. Abi-Jaber, professor of government at Smith College, best described the Arab reaction to Israeli policies: "The Israelis have systematically pursued an expansionist policy and Israeli leaders are fond of stating their militant belief that the Arabs 'understand only the language of force.'"[2] Thus, while Israel defended her policies by citing the need to maintain her security, the Arabs saw these measures in terms of an Israeli expansionist policy designed to take over additional Arab lands. This Arab fear of Israel expansion at their expense is readily apparent upon examination of the obvious Israeli motives for their preemptive strike of June 5, 1967, leading to the 1967 Six-Day War.

Israel had claimed that she was threatened with extermination. However, an article in the daily newspaper of the Israeli Labor party of June 10, 1972, reported a debate between Israeli generals Weizman, Govich, Peled, and Herzog in which all were agreed that Israel had been in no danger of extinction before it launched its preemptive strike. This fact—coupled with the Israeli demand for retention of the territories it had conquered, based upon a "continuing threat" to the security and existence of the state of Israel—led the Arabs to believe that the preemptive strike could have had only one goal: expansion.[3]

Moreover, the Arabs saw the Israeli policy of calling for increased immigration to Israel, together with the Israelis' speedy attempt to establish settlements in the occupied territories and to populate those settlements with the new Jewish immigrants, as an organized, sustained, and generously financed plan of continuing Israeli expansion. The Arabs considered these Israeli policies a fundamental obstacle to any enduring peace.[4] After listening to Israeli Prime Minister Golda Meir's territorial demands of March 13, 1971—upon which Israel's acceptance of peace in the Middle East was conditional—Egypt's ambassador to the United States, Ashraf Ghorbal, remarked, "It is not peace she is after, not freedom of navigation, but simply territory. She is creating a new map for Israel and she is asking us to negotiate our territory to create that map."[5] Moreover, Israeli Defense Minister Moshe Dayan did much to give the Arab fear of Israeli expansion a solid foundation after the 1967 war when he told the youth of the United Labor party of Israel that: "Another generation will take the frontiers to where they belong."[6] This statement, taken together with Israel's territorial demands and with continuing Israeli settlement in the occupied territories, made it very hard to escape the conclusion drawn by Egyptian President Nasser that the Israeli raison d'être was expansion.[7]

With the Israeli fear for their security on the one hand and the Arab fear of Israeli expansion on the other, the Arabs found themselves in a very frustrating position. This position was noted by Roger Fisher, Harvard professor of international law, in his testimony before the House Foreign Affairs Subcommittee on the Near East.

> The Egyptians are in a very frustrating position. The more they threaten action against Israel for failure to withdraw, the less Israel wants to withdraw. The Israelis say to themselves "If there is going to be a war, let's have it at Suez and not at Gaza." Then if the Egyptians do not threaten the Israelis relax and say "There is no reason to withdraw. Everything is fine as it is. Let's let the situation develop until the Arabs become more reasonable. The longer we hold onto their land the more reasonable they will get. Let's not withdraw.[8]

Thus, the Israelis as victors and occupants of the Arab lands conquered in 1967 held the upper hand. If the Arabs did nothing, the Israelis refused to withdraw, waiting for the Arabs to capitulate to an Israeli-imposed settlement which involved retention of most, if not all, the occupied territories. If the Arabs threatened renewed armed conflict, the Israelis consolidated their holdings, citing the need to protect themselves and their preference to do any fighting outside of Israel proper and within the occupied territories.

The Arabs saw their own fear of Israeli expansionism made manifest in the Israeli policies of occupation, particularly in the Gaza Strip. Here, as in the other occupied territories (see chapter 6), the Arab people were subjected to the destruction of their homes and villages, and they and their families were forcibly deported, while their lands were settled by Jewish immigrants. Hence there was a change in the geographic structure and the demographic composition of the occupied territories.[9]

Another Israeli demand—that for direct negotiations between the Israelis and the Arabs—the Arabs compared to a conqueror meeting the conquered to discuss the fruits of conquest.[10] But Egypt agreed to such talks without prior conditions. Saying on the one hand that everything was negotiable, Israel demanded to retain parts of Egypt, Jordan, and Syria which were being occupied and she refused to withdraw any forces pending a negotiated settlement. These Israeli preconditions were seen as a peace diktat imposed by the victor upon the vanquished, a system which the United Nations Charter had outlawed.[11] Egyptian President Nasser, in proposing conditions for peace which he felt the Israelis might accept, said, "I want a settlement with Israel, but not unconditional surrender. So far, Israel has offered us terms of surrender."[12]

In essence, the Arabs refused direct negotiations on Israel's terms for the same reason that Israel had proposed them. In direct negotiations Israel had the advantage of playing out to the full the weight of a military occupation, while the Arabs were unable to use their economic and political influence throughout the world. Despite all of their failures and difficulties, however, the Arabs refused to be forced into surrender.[13]

Shortly after the fighting ceased in 1967, Arab leaders held a summit conference at Khartoum. Israel took that conference and loudly proclaimed its results, out of context, to justify her need to maintain occupation of the Arab territories seized during the 1967 war. Israel termed the decisions to be (1) no recognition of Israel, (2) no negotiations with her, (3) no peace treaty.[14] The inference was obvious: The Arabs *do not* want peace. Quite the contrary, however, at Khartoum, Arab leaders agreed to seek a peaceful, political settlement with Israel rather than a military one. Such settlement was to be based on substantive help from the United Nations or some other third party. Although the three important Arab conditions had indeed been the ones emphasized by Israel, the Arab stand was prompted by Israel's consolidation of her grip on the occupied territories. This made the Arabs apprehensive of direct negotiations and legal recognition of Israel, for fear that such actions would enable Israel to gain some legal status in the occupied territories prior to her withdrawal from those territories.[15] Hence, prior to the outbreak of hostilities in 1973, Israel had maintained a position of closing the door to all solutions except capitulation and acceptance of Israeli diktat.[16]

The Arabs made a significant policy shift in their response

to United Nations Ambassador Gunnar Jarring's aide-mémoire by accepting direct negotiations with Israel and ending their state of belligerency, but they expressed the view that a lasting peace could not be realized without Israel's withdrawal from all occupied Arab territories. Israel, however, refused to relent in its demand to retain at least some of the occupied territories for security purposes, despite appeals by Secretary-General U Thant and the United States. Israeli refusal to withdraw from the occupied territories brought the Jarring talks to a grinding halt.[17]

The principal goal of the Arabs in a negotiated settlement was to secure withdrawal by Israel from all the occupied territories. This policy is in line with that proposed by William Rogers when he was United States secretary of state in 1969. It required Israeli withdrawal from captured Arab territories to the frontiers that had existed before June 5, 1967, with only "insubstantial" changes in the boundaries, "not reflecting the weight of conquest."[18] However, based on continued Israeli demands for substantial boundary changes and retention of most, if not all, of the occupied territories, the Arabs saw that, left to themselves, the Israelis would not withdraw from the occupied Arab territories.[19]

The Arab countries saw a contradiction in American support of Security Council Resolution 242 (1967) and its continued support of Israeli occupation. The Arabs took the United States' statement that Israel should not withdraw from the occupied territories before a settlement was reached to mean a settlement unfavorable to the Arabs, since Israel had the whip hand.[20] They also saw Israel's refusal to accept anything less than its demands for a settlement which included retention of most, if not all, of the occupied territories as being due principally to American military support, which allowed Israel to maintain its occupation, and to American political support, which protected Israel against any United Nations action.[21] They saw American military aid to Israel not only as defending Israel's conquests but also as making possible Israel's further and repeated military strikes against its Arab neighbors, such as Israeli military incursions into Lebanon and air raids against Syria and Egypt. In addition, they saw American military aid to Israel as encouraging Israel to maintain her attitude of arrogance and defiance in the face of worldwide reprobation.[22] Finally, they saw the American request for the Arabs to negotiate while their lands remained occupied as a request for the Arabs to accept a settlement under duress.[23]

The Arab states saw the Israeli quest for security as being achieved at the expense of Arab security. Thus, the perpetuation of Israeli superiority in armaments was seen as insuring that the Arabs would never be able to regain any territory that Israel might decide it needs.[24] Moreover, the Arabs did not see additional Israeli security as coming from the annexation of additional territories. Instead, they saw security for the entire Middle East as coming from a peaceful settlement in which the nature of the relationship between the two sides was changed.[25]

Continued Israeli occupation, the annexation of Jerusalem, the mistreatment of the Arab population in the occupied territories, all these things—in spite of numerous resolutions by the United Nations condemning these actions—led the Arabs to the conclusion that the United Nations and its Charter were irrelevant to the Israelis. Hence, Israeli actions were seen as being outside the United Nations, outside the Charter, and outside international law.[26]

No matter what position was taken with regard to the conflict in the Middle East, the following facts were clear: (1) Arab territory was being occupied by Israeli forces; (2) the United Nations resolution of December 13, 1971, called for Israeli withdrawal; (3) Israel not only refused to withdraw but established numerous Jewish settlements on land in the occupied territories which it had expropriated from its Arab owners, who were forced to leave because of Israel's oppressive measures; (4) the United Nations had been prevented from taking effective measures in accordance with Chapter VII of the Charter to remedy the situation principally because of United States efforts to substitute political expediency for the rule of international law;

(5) all the above factors point to one conclusion: namely, resistance.[27]

Israel's refusal to withdraw from the occupied territories voluntarily or in response to a United Nations resolution calling for their withdrawal led the Arab governments to believe that only military defeat or strong external pressure from the United Nations and from the Big Four (United States, Russia, Great Britain, and France) would ever persuade the Israelis to withdraw.[28] Israel's constant use of force in violation of international law and the international community's indulgence of Israel's flaunting the law left the Arabs little recourse except to fight.[29] Explaining the Arab position before the United Nations General Assembly, Egyptian Foreign Minister Mohammed H. El-Zayyat said, "We refuse, however, to be dictated to, subjected to long occupation and we refuse to stay occupied."[30] Thus, the Arabs felt that the persistent inability of the United Nations to uphold the principles of the Charter that were being violated by Israel allowed them to take every possible means to restore their rights and integrity in the occupied territories under Article 51 of the Charter.[31]

In an attempt to get at Palestinian commandos, Israel made a number of large-scale military attacks on Arab towns and refugee camps in Lebanon and Syria. The Arabs looked at those actions and wondered what the Jewish and world reactions would have been if, during the latter years of the British mandate in Palestine, the British had used planes and artillery to attack Tel Aviv and other Jewish communities in the Palestine area because of Jewish terrorism in Palestine.[32]

In essence, the Arabs saw Israeli justification for their actions following their preemptive strike against Egyptian air bases on June 5, 1967, as being a theory of territorial expansion in which any state wishing to expand need only invade a neighboring state, occupy its territory and impose its territorial demands by means of superior force, and then proclaim that it has the natural right to hold that territory because this has been done by other states in past history or that it has a historical right to hold the territory because their ancestors held it ages ago. The Arabs attack this Israeli theory of territorial expansion by noting that the United Nations produced more advanced principles of international law, which made expansion by force illegal for all United Nations members.[33]

Thus, the Arabs viewed continuing Israeli occupation as a sad heritage of the pre-Charter era, showing a failure to understand that the world as a whole can never live half free and strong and half subjugated and poor. The Arab hope for the future was best expressed by Egyptian Foreign Minister El-Zayyat, who said, "For centuries in the past, nations have been subjected to the misery brought about by violence. We all look ahead now to a world advancing in peace and under the protection of the law. Let us make it absolutely impossible for anyone to live outside that law."[34]

10

The Ever-Changing United States Position on the Middle East

The position of the United States in the Middle East conflict has seemed to change with the changes of administrations, while the conflict continues in various stages with differing amounts of actual fighting. In 1956, for example, Israel, Great Britain, and France invaded Egypt, and Israel occupied much the same land then as it did following the 1967 war. The United States joined with the Soviet Union in pressuring Israel to withdraw to the frontiers it had had before the hostilities began, following the principle which prevented the acquisition of territory by war.[1]

As the 1967 war broke out in the Middle East, the major goal of the American delegation was a return by both sides, principally the Israelis, to the pre-June status quo. However, less than a week after the cease-fire was effected, White House "sources" considered the American pledge to support the "territorial integrity of all nations" to be flexible enough to allow Israel to acquire buffer zones to "protect" herself from her neighbors. A return to the prewar boundaries was considered by American officials to be a "prescription for renewed hostilities." Moreover, by mid-June 1967, American Ambassador to the United Nations Arthur Goldberg was stating that unless the Arabs were to agree to Israel's demands, Israel must retain whatever territory she had conquered. Thus, the American commitment to preserve the status quo of Israeli occupation of Arab territories worked only to the advantage of Israel and in support of Israel's intention to maintain and consolidate its claims to territories occupied by force.[2]

On the one hand, as late as July 14, 1967, Ambassador Goldberg said, "One immediate, obvious and imperative step is the disengagement of all forces and the withdrawal of Israeli forces to their own territory."[3] On the other hand, however, the United States was implicitly but vigorously arguing that Israel was entitled to occupy the captured Arab territories until a comprehensive settlement was reached between the parties. The American position was taken because American leaders felt that the Israeli military advantage should be exploited to achieve a comprehensive and reliable peace settlement.[4] The American position was also due to American preoccupation with Vietnam and with its conflict with the Soviet Union on that and other problems as well as to American vulnerability to domestic Zionist pressures. Hence, the Soviet Union and the United States backed opposing sides in 1967, and a withdrawal like the one in 1956, when the super powers had taken a common position, was prevented.[5]

On December 9, 1969, Secretary of State William Rogers announced a plan for peace which seemed to indicate a substantial shift in United States policy toward the conflict. The Rogers proposal stated that any territorial changes should be confined to insubstantial border alterations along the Israeli-Egyptian border. In addition, any border alterations made should not reflect the weight of conquest.[6] In theory, at least, the United States had shifted its policy from support of Israeli demands for peace to the position called for by the international law of no territorial acquisitions by war.

Even though, in theory, American policy had shifted to a position more favorable to the Arabs, in fact American policy remained the same. This continuing American policy in favor of Israel can be seen most clearly by the continuation of American military aid to Israel even though Israel had flatly rejected both American and United Nations peace proposals, and, as its conditions for peace, had insisted on direct negotiations between the parties and ultimate Israeli retention of most, if not all, of the occupied territories.[7]

An August 1973 speech before the General Assembly by American Ambassador to the United Nations John Scali showed another shift in American policy, in theory, concerning the Middle East. Offering a different American interpretation of Security Council Resolution 242, Ambassador Scali said,

> One aspect of [the Middle East] problem is the question of boundaries. There are many strongly held views about where final boundaries between Israel and its neighbors should be drawn. Resolution 242 has often been cited to support one view or another. But the fact is that Resolution 242 is silent on the specific question of where the final border should be located. It neither endorses nor precludes—let me repeat *neither endorses nor precludes*—the armistice lines which existed between Israel, Egypt, Jordan and Syria on June 4, 1967, as the final, secure and recognized boundaries.[8]

This statement seems to indicate that Israel is not precluded from expanding her borders to meet her security requirements, despite the principle in international law which prohibits the acquisition of territory by war. This is a significant shift from "insubstantial border changes not reflecting the weight of conquest."

The importance of American military, economic, and political support of Israel can be seen on both sides of the Arab-Israeli conflict. While the Israelis call for additional support to bolster their military and economy,[9] the Arabs make the cautious guess that without American military, economic, and political support, the Zionist establishment in the Middle East could not get very far by going it alone.[10]

Thus, American theoretical policy was in a constant state of flux, while policy in fact was a mere reversal of that prior to 1967. American policy in theory and fact in 1956 required Israeli withdrawal to the borders it had before the hostilities began. In 1967 American policy in theory reversed itself, supporting Israeli occupation until a settlement satisfactory to Israel was reached by negotiations between the parties. In 1969 this policy in theory reversed itself again by requiring insubstantial territorial changes "not reflecting the weight of conquest," and in 1973 it was reversed yet again, by inferring allowance under Resolution 242 of Israeli acquisition of territory. However, American policy in fact was a mere reversal of what it had been in 1956, when the United States exerted pressure that caused Israeli withdrawal. American political, economic, and military aid perpetuated Israeli occupation of the Arab territories captured in 1967, despite the requirements by international law that Israel withdraw.

11

The Yom Kippur War—1973

On the afternoon of October 6, 1973, on the Jewish holiday of Yom Kippur, or the Day of Atonement, conflicting radio reports came out of Egypt, Syria, and Israel. One thing was certain. The fourth Arab-Israeli war in twenty-five years was underway. The Egyptians reported that the Israelis had attacked Egyptian forces at Za'faranah and Sukhnah using a number of air formations, while the Israeli Navy approached positions from the Gulf of Suez. At the same time, Radio Damascus reported that Egyptian and Syrian positions along the 1967 cease-fire line had been attacked by Israeli soldiers. Israel denied both reports, claiming instead that Egypt and Syria had attacked her forces in the occupied territories.[1]

Once again, the world community was faced with the question of who had started the hostilities. United Nations truce observers reported to New York that at the Golan Heights and the Suez Canal, Egyptian and Syrian troops were the ones to first cross the cease-fire line.[2] Nothing was reported by the observers to either dispute or verify the claims coming from Cairo and Radio Damascus. There had been reports of a military buildup in the Arab sector in the days preceding the initiation of hostilities, but such a buildup had gone largely unnoticed. The fighting in the initial stages of the war was intense, and the casualties on both sides were reported heavy.[3]

At an emergency meeting of the United Nations Security Council, the question of who was to blame for the hostilities went largely ignored except for a few political remarks. The consensus of opinion was, not to apportion blame, but to seek an immediate end to the hostilities and to deal with the problems of the Middle East through the framework of Security Council Resolution 242 of November 1967. John Scali of the United States advised the Council to avoid trying to assess blame and to concentrate on three goals which would help in attaining a real peace: (1) an end to the current fighting; (2) a return by both sides to their respective positions before the fighting broke out; and (3) an agreement by the parties involved on the validity of past United Nations resolutions on the Middle East, including Resolution 242. Sir Donald Maitland of the United Kingdom suggested an urgent call for the cessation of hostilities and the use of those tragic events as a catalyst for a fresh peace effort on the basis of Resolution 242. Representative Louis de Guiringaud of France noted that the main obstacle to a negotiated settlement based on Resolution 242 was the continued Israeli occupation of the Arab territories taken during the 1967 war.[4]

At this point, it is interesting to analyze the United States position on ending the war. That position was outlined by Secretary of State Henry Kissinger at a news conference on October 25, 1973, in which he indicated that two major problems existed. First was the problem of ending the hostilities as soon as possible. Second was ending the hostilities in such a manner as to remove the conditions that had produced four wars in the Middle East in twenty-five years. From there, Dr. Kissinger went on to emphasize that the conditions which had produced the Yom Kippur War could not be permitted to continue.[5] Egypt's President Sadat made similar remarks in an address to his parliament on October 16, 1973, and Jordan's King Hussein echoed those remarks at a news conference on October 17, 1973, in which he noted that Israel wanted to have both peace and the occupied territories, and they would have to choose between the two.[6]

After extensive debate on the situation in the Middle East, the United Nations Security Council passed Resolution 338, which required the parties to the conflict to do the following:

1. cease all fighting and terminate all military activity immediately at the positions they currently occupied

2. immediately after the cease-fire, start implementation of Resolution 242
3. commence negotiations aimed at establishing a just and lasting peace for the area.[7]

Even if, at this point, the reader decides to place the blame for the 1973 Yom Kippur War on the Egyptians and Syrians, he should examine and reexamine the actions of the Israelis during their occupation of the territories taken during the 1967 war. Such an examination will show the frustrations the Arabs have experienced with Israel occupation.

United Nations Security Council Resolution 242 emphasized the "inadmissibility of the acquisition of territory by war. . . ." Yet no sooner had the fighting stopped in the 1967 war than—despite declarations that Israel had no territorial ambitions in the region—the Israeli parliament legislated a "reunification" of the city of Jerusalem, annexing the Arab portion of the city, and destroyed the Arab villages of Imwas, Beit Nuba, and Yalu in the Latrun area, expelling all Arab inhabitants.[8] In the city of Jerusalem alone, some 4,000 Arabs had lost their homes before the end of June 1967. By January 1968, Israeli authorities had expropriated more than 800 acres of land in the Arab sector of Jerusalem and had announced plans for the construction of housing estates on the slopes of Mount Scopus, overlooking the Old City.[9] These actions continued despite protests from Arab leaders and from the United Nations. In fact, the United Nations General Assembly declared Israeli actions "invalid" in a resolution dated July 4, 1967. At the same time, the Israelis, despite their "establishment of open borders," permitted only 14,000 refugees to reenter the territories, out of 150,000 applications filed with the Red Cross.[10] The Israelis used the new housing built in occupied territories for new Jewish immigrants and began the preparation and publication of a "master plan" whereby the Jewish population would be doubled by 1980, with an eventual total of 900,000.[11]

On the West Bank, the Israelis expropriated some 65,000 acres of land, which they held through the Custodian of Abandoned Property. The occupiers did set up a committee to handle claims and / or disputes, but the decision of the committee was final. Protests were dealt with in terms of the British mandate, in which homes of "suspected saboteurs" were demolished and numerous persons were arrested.[12] The expropriation of lands by the Israelis provided the impetus for the Palestinian organization's rise to acceptance in the world community. It is one thing to destroy something under the guise of law and protection. It is a far more serious thing, however, when the Israelis take the land of the occupied territories, build settlements on it, and use those settlements solely to house new Jewish immigrants, while the old Arab owners are either arrested or herded into refugee camps. This type of activity is certainly not supportive of the principle of the inadmissibility of territory taken by war. There is only one term for such a policy—expansionism. At the same time, despite international law in the form of resolutions by the United Nations Security Council, political realities showed that the Israelis were still going about taking Arab lands in the occupied territories and building settlements for their citizens on those lands.

In the Gaza Strip, the Arabs charged that the Israelis were compelling residents to leave their homes and expropriating their lands. The Israelis responded by stating that the residents had not been permitted to leave during the twenty years of Egyptian rule and that those residents now had "freedom of movement." The question becomes one of what the actual difference is between the terms "freedom of movement" and "forced evacuation." The Israelis attributed the increased movement out of the region to the precarious economic and security situation in Jordan, but no specifics were given.[13]

In January 1970 Israel launched a series of massive bombing attacks against Egypt, with three goals: (1) to force the Egyptians to respect the cease-fire; (2) to prevent Egyptian preparations for a new war; and (3) to weaken the Egyptian regime. In point of fact, the bombing raids had three results, but they were totally opposite the original goals of those attacks: (1) the raids, which caused heavy civilian casualties, strengthened the Egyptian government; (2) the raids damaged Israel's image in the outside world; and (3) the raids drew the Soviet Union into the picture as a supplier to Egypt. At the same time, although both Egypt and Jordan accepted the proposals of United States Secretary of State William Rogers for the implementation of Resolution 242, the Israelis maintained the position that no withdrawal would take place until a peace treaty had been signed.[14] With the acceptance of the Rogers plan by King Hussein of Jordan, civil war with the Popular Front for the Liberation of Palestine became inevitable late in 1970. Egyptian President Nasser successfully negotiated a cease-fire after ten days of bitter fighting, but he died the day after the cease-fire. Once again, division over how to handle the Israeli occupation disrupted the Arab world, this time leading to civil war in Jordan. Yet the Israeli position remained firm and was enforced by incursions into Lebanon twice in 1972 and in early 1973. Israeli raids did little more than add to the suffering of the civilian population in Lebanon.

The greatest source of frustration leading to the 1973 Yom Kippur War was the establishment of Israeli settlements in the occupied territories. Some fifty settlements had been established by the fall of 1973 (the number would increase to more than ninety by June 1978[15]), and the Israeli government expressed confidence in their military superiority over the Arabs. The Israelis had totally ignored United Nations resolutions calling for withdrawal from the occupied territories. Among the Israeli leaders asserting the "right of settlement" and calling for increased settlement as a "security measure" was one Menachem Begin, at that time a member of the minority party and a minister without portfolio.[16] Some of the settlements had interesting beginnings. For instance, in April 1968 a group of religious Jews had rented a hotel in the occupied territories and gathered there to celebrate the Passover. After the holiday had concluded, some of the members of the group announced their intention to remain in the territory and to settle there, even though such settlement had not been approved.[17] These actions on the part of Israeli citizens and their government, as well as the failure on the part of the international community to stop such actions (despite the fact that such actions clearly violated the accepted principle of international law that territories could no longer be conquered in or by war), gave the Arab community a sense of frustration and hopelessness which culminated in the 1973 Yom Kippur War.

In an interesting side note, the Israelis have contended that they should be permitted to retain the Arab territories taken during the 1967 war because that territory was taken in an action of self-defense. Such an argument assumes that the Israeli action in 1967 *was* indeed self-defense when, in point of fact, it *was not* self-defense. The Israeli sinking of the U.S.S. *Liberty*, a spy ship which was off the Mediterranean coast and in a position to see the Israeli attack, proves that the Israeli attack was not in self-defense in 1967. More recently, the Israelis have admitted that their actions in 1967 came before Arab reaction, but they now call their actions preemptive strikes, in an attempt to justify them. Such an argument does, of course, make the occupation of Arab territories illegal. At the same time, it could also be interpreted as justifying the use of force to liberate the occupied territories, in that self-defense is not inconsistent with the United Nations Charter.[18] That is not to say that the Arabs should immediately arm themselves and attack the Israeli outposts, as they attempted to do in 1973. Suffice it to say that international law and its various principles can be used to justify many "interesting" actions. In reality, the more realistic approach would be to follow Security Council Resolution 242 by promoting peace and denying any benefits of war in the form of conquered territories.

The effect of the 1973 Yom Kippur War upon events and policies in the Middle East was incredible. To begin with, despite the final military outcome, the Egyptians and Syrians achieved sufficient military successes during the initial days of the war to crush the myth that wide buffer zones would be sufficient to protect Israel from attack or that the Israeli army was sufficiently strong for the Israelis to ignore world opinion.[19]

At the same time, Arab solidarity was developed, and for the first time, the Arabs used their oil as a political tool by stopping oil exports to Western nations supporting Israel. Moreover, Israel's policy of creeping annexation had been brought to light, which weakened the Israeli position and eventually resulted in an Arab-American reconciliation.[20]

In addition, several new leaders emerged on the Arab front as a result of the 1973 war. King Faisal of Saudi Arabia emerged as an Arab spokesman, and through his efforts, with the assistance of Henry Kissinger, small but important Israeli withdrawals were obtained.[21]

The most remarkable change occurred in world opinion concerning the Palestinians, as led by the Palestinian Liberation Organization. Before the 1973 war, the world image of the PLO had been extremely poor in light of the skyjackings and terrorist attacks in the early 1970s and the attack on the Israeli Olympic team in Munich in 1972. With the 1973 war, the world community realized that the central issue of the Middle East situation was the question of the rights of the Palestinian people. In November 1973, the leaders of Arab governments endorsed the PLO as the "sole legitimate representative of the Palestinian people." On September 21, 1974, the United Nations General Assembly voted for the first time since the establishment of the state of Israel in 1948 to include the Palestinian question on its agenda for discussion and debate. This recognition culminated in the October 14 invitation to the PLO by the General Assembly to take part in the debate.[22]

Arab diplomacy continued to gather momentum during 1975, with a second disengagement agreement between Egypt and Israel, whereby Egypt got the return of the Abu Rudais oil fields. At the same time, the United Nations General Assembly adopted three resolutions favoring the Palestinians and their position on Middle Eastern affairs. The first, Resolution 3236, established a twenty-nation committee to work out plans for the implementation of the Palestinian right to self-determination and national independence. The second resolution invited the PLO to take part in all future UN debates on the Middle East. The third resolution denounced Zionism as a form of racism and racial discrimination. At the same time, the United States was forced to use its veto to prevent a resolution censuring Israel for a series of severe air raids over Lebanon, in which seventy-five persons were killed. The United States also had to use its veto to overturn resolutions condemning Israeli settlements in the occupied territories and establishing the right of the Palestinians to establish their own state.[23]

Resolution 3236 of the United Nations General Assembly is important in that it does the following:

1. Reaffirms the inalienable rights of the Palestinian people in Palestine, including: (a) the right to self-determination without external interference; (b) the right to national independence and sovereignty;
2. Reaffirms also the inalienable right of the Palestinians to return to their homes and property, from which they have been displaced and uprooted, and calls for their return;
3. Emphasizes that full respect for, and the realization of, these inalienable rights of the Palestinian people are indispensable for the solution of the question of Palestine;
4. Recognizes the Palestinian people as a principal party in the establishment of a just and durable peace in the Middle East;
5. Further recognizes the right of the Palestinians to regain their rights by all means in accordance with the purposes and principles of the Charter of the United Nations;
6. Appeals to all states and international organizations to extend their support to the Palestinian people in the struggle to restore their rights, in accordance with the Charter;
7. Requests the secretary-general to establish contacts with the Palestinian Liberation Organization on all matters concerning the question of Palestine;
8. Requests the secretary-general to report to the General Assembly at its thirtieth session on the implementation of the present resolution;
9. Decides to include the item entitled "Question of Palestine" in the provisional agenda of its thirtieth session.

As a result of this resolution, the Palestine Liberation Organization achieved the status of "quasi-statehood."[24] Such a status gives rise to international rights and duties under international law.

Yet despite this new role for the PLO, many of the underlying problems remain, as the Israeli occupation continues, along with the implementation of new settlements in the occupied territories. Although such problems continue to be a prime source of frustration, the quest for peace remained strong in one Anwar Sadat, president of Egypt.

12

Some Conclusions

One of the main reasons for the lengthy conflict between the Arabs and the Israelis stemmed from the fact that the Israelis refused to believe that their right violated other rights belonging to the Arabs, which were no less respectable.[1] This can be seen in the context of a conversation between Secretary of State Henry Kissinger and a personal friend of his, who happened to be the Israeli general who had captured Jordanian Jerusalem during the 1967 war. The Israeli general saw no time limit to Israeli occupation of Arab territories captured in 1967, which he said were being held to bring the Arabs into negotiation and to conclude a contractual peace which would guarantee Israel the security she sought. Kissinger argued that eventually world opinion would force Israel to reconsider that position. Finally, the general asked Kissinger what alternative there was to Israel's position that would guarantee the objectives Israel was after. Kissinger replied that the question before Israel was whether she could trade some of her superiority for some political legitimacy.[2] Thus, the question of the military security of Israel, who has proven she can dominate her neighbors militarily without international guarantees, should not obscure other issues in the dispute.[3]

One of the major issues, which in the past had been obscured by the Israeli cry for her security, was the application of international law to the resolution of the Arab-Israeli conflict. The importance of international law was pointed out in the remark quoted above by President Dwight D. Eisenhower: "There can be no peace—without law. And there can be no law—if we were to invoke one code of international conduct for those who oppose us and another for our friends."[4] Hence, the importance of international law remains its ability to insure peace in international relations. Its application and enforcement in the Middle East conflict is the only way to insure a lasting peace.

Israeli interpretations of international law in practice were based on "classical" concepts. One such concept allows the use of the preemptive strike as a means of attacking and defeating an enemy before he attacks you. However, modern concepts of international law as implied from Articles 2(4) and 51 of the United Nations Charter have sharply restricted a state's traditional right of self-defense. The basic modern rule is that a state may have recourse to armed force only in response to a first use of armed force by another state or international entity.[5] Thus, the use of the preemptive strike is forbidden under modern international law. Israel also looked to its rights of occupation and annexation in terms of classical international law. Under classical international law a state victorious in armed confrontation against another state could occupy lands of the defeated state. Moreover, the fruits-of-conquest theory allowed the victorious state to annex lands and to take whatever steps were necessary to prevent the rise of the conditions which had led to the confrontation. Thus, under the classical theory, the victorious Romans salted the ruins of Carthage, the victorious Greeks burned Troy, and Attila the Hun ravaged western Europe. On the other hand, modern international law recognizes the inherent sovereignty and territorial integrity of states, and the principle of the inadmissibility of the acquisition of territory by war was therefore formulated. Thus, under modern international law, the territorial sovereignty of states exists where the boundaries are currently located. Those boundaries are considered permanent, and additional land can be acquired only by treaty between two consenting states in an equal bargaining position. Therefore, no territory can be acquired by conquest, and treaties ceding land cannot reflect the weight of conquest.

Throughout this volume, constant reference has been made to Israeli control of the media, which allowed only their side of the confrontation to be seen, and the Israeli propaganda campaign of 1967 to brand Egypt as the aggressor in the 1967 war. The importance of this can be seen in the fact that in almost every analysis available in the United States on the Middle East conflict, the writer presupposed either that Israel had been fully justified in 1967 in the use of force against Egypt, Syria, and Jordan or that she had been at least sufficiently justified to attack first. Thus, on the assumption that Israel acted in self-defense, her occupation of the Arab territory became justified.[6]

American acceptance of the Israeli point of view was based on Israel's being portrayed as a pro-Western, democratic country highly developed in technology. Moreover, the Israelis' race brought back memories of Jewish sufferings at the hand of Hitler and immediately created both sympathy for the Jewish cause and a fear of being branded anti-Semitic. However, the danger of a continuing belief that the Israelis can do no wrong comes when justification of Israeli actions is attempted also for the severe measures of expropriation of Arab lands, expulsion of Arab inhabitants from those lands, and establishment of Jewish settlements in the occupied territories—which boils down to saying that the end justifies the means.

International law and the knowledge of the existence of Israeli propaganda can both be considered through a determination of the legal status of Israel in the occupied Arab territories. Two questions were posed in chapter 3 in this regard. The first question dealt with whether or not Israel was a legal occupant or an invader-occupant. The status of legal occupant would be accorded an occupying power who had captured the enemy's territory as a result of a defensive action in response to an attack. Under modern international law, a legal occupant is entitled to international recognition of his occupation and does not have to withdraw until a formal peace treaty ends the hostilities. Thus, it became important for Israel to make the international community think that her actions in 1967 were defensive, even by means of a propaganda campaign blaming the 1967 war on Egypt. Once Israel had consolidated her occupation of the Arab territories through the establishment of numerous settlements and with the full support of the United States, what the remainder of the international community felt no longer mattered. The propaganda campaign was then dropped, and the truth leaked out about Israeli actions in 1967 and afterwards. Had Israel immediately been branded the aggressor, as she had been in 1956, her position following the 1967 war would have been identified as that of invader-occupant. Such status would have forbidden international recognition, prevented the occupant from achieving any type of sovereignty in the occupied territories, and required immediate withdrawal without conditions, as in 1956. International opinion is equally important in answering the second question, which is whether or not the international community approves of the Israeli actions taken in 1967 so that Israel would be allowed the benefits of the status of legal occupant. As mentioned above, the United Nations finally passed a resolution in December 1971 which demanded Israeli withdrawal from the occupied territories. Moreover, the nonaligned members of the United Nations have called for Israeli withdrawal, as has the Soviet Union.[7] Thus, Israel's failure to win international approval for her continued occupation prevented her from achieving the status of legal occupant in the occupied territories, and she should be denied the benefits accruing from that status.

United Nations resolutions must be interpreted within the context of United Nations Charter principles, declarations of the organization, and international obligations in conventions and international rules. Thus, United Nations Security Council Resolution 242 must be referred specifically to Article 2 of the Charter, which prevents "the threat or use of force against the territorial integrity of any state."[8] Resolution 242 must also be interpreted in light of the Declaration on the Strengthening of International Security and the Declaration on Principles of Friendly Relations among States, both of which adhere to the modern international legal principle of the inadmissibility of the acquisition of territory by war. Whether or not such declarations and resolutions are legally binding, they have great political and moral significance in international relations.[9]

Looking directly at Resolution 242, two limitations on the Arab-Israeli conflict are noteworthy. First, the principle of

Israeli withdrawal from the occupied territories is connected to the principle of "termination of all claims or status of belligerency and respect for and acknowledgment of the sovereignty, territorial integrity and political independence of every state in the area. . . ."[10] Through the Arabs' acceptance of the proposal in the aide-mémoire of Gunnar Jarring, they have complied fully with the latter of these provisions. The Israelis, however, did not withdraw from the occupied territories. Moreover, the Israeli demand for "secure and recognized borders" is limited by "the inadmissibility of the acquisition of territory by war."[11] Once again, Israeli retention of the occupied territories cannot be justified under modern international law.

The Israeli occupation of the Arab territories was itself governed by a different set of principles in international law, including the Hague Convention IV of 1907, the London Charter of 1949, and the Geneva Convention IV of 1949 on the Protection of Civilians in Occupied Territories. These international legal rules prohibit the destruction or expropriation of private property, the forced transfer of the civilian population outside the occupied area, and the settlement within the occupied territories of nationals of the occupying power. Yet, following the 1967 war, Israel spent some 280,000,000 Israeli pounds in its program of expropriation of Arab lands in the occupied territories, expulsion of Arab inhabitants, and establishment of Jewish settlements. This program of changing the geographic composition and demographic structure had its purpose: to make annexation of the occupied Arab territories easier. Periodic censures by the United Nations Human Rights Commission have done little to slow the pace of this Israeli type of expansion.

Although Israel attempted to justify its presence in the occupied Arab territories to the outside world by arguing its need for security and its ever-present fear of destruction by the Arabs, the Israelis pacified their own consciences by referring to the argument used by Zionist leader Rupin, who in 1928 said, "the same right which entitles the Arabs to remain here entitles us to come."[12] In chapter 7 the question was posed as to whether or not Israel had gone beyond her security requirements in her territorial demands and had become bent on expansion.

Prior to the end of the 1967 war, Israel made no complaint about a general Arab danger to her security. If there had been an actual fear for her existence immediately prior to the 1967 war, Israel had had adequate opportunity to allow the United Nations Emergency Force troops to move across the Egyptian border into her territory rather than letting them return home. Moreover, in October 1966 the Israeli representative to the United Nations remarked before the General Assembly that Israel had no security problems with the Arabs and that she recognized her 1949 borders as being immune from change without consent. After 1967, however, Israel's demand for security implied the need for more territory, that territory which she had occupied. It is essential to remember that the territory occupied by Israel is four times the size of Israel's area before the 1967 hostilities. Inasmuch as Israel had no security problems until she began to occupy captured Arab territories equivalent to four times her original size, retention of those territories was more in the interest of Zionist expansion than security. Moreover, the fact that justifications for settlements in the occupied territories were based more on historical considerations than on security requirements adds to the conclusion that the basis for retention of the occupied territories was the desire for expansion.

While Israel constantly called for direct negotiations, the Arabs saw this as an attempt by her to achieve a legitimate status in the occupied territories. This would have come about because Israel demanded nearly all of the occupied territories as a settlement, while the Arabs had nothing to bargain with. Israeli refusal to accept anything less was based on the belief that the United States would back her no matter what position she took.[13]

Arab frustrations and inability to bring about an end to Israeli occupation in the occupied territories finally culminated in the Egyptian-Syrian offensive in October 1973. Yet despite a united Arab front and their use of the oil embargo, Israeli consolidation of the occupied territories and American aid proved too much for the Arabs to handle and led to further Arab defeats and the loss of additional Arab territories.

In this series of Arab-Israeli wars which were fought for

twenty-five years, the Israeli military victory has been more sensational and the Arab military defeat more shattering in each successive bout of the struggle between the two. Still, a military defeat, however severe and humiliating, is not decisive unless it puts the defeated state out of action permanently, and a military victory, however overwhelming, is like gold—it is worth only what the victor is able to purchase with it. If the victor cannot purchase something he needs, the victory is merely a "wasting asset." The Israelis have failed in each instance to convert a military victory into the intrinsically valuable commodity of peace that they need.[14] Hence, the lesson of 1967 is that military victory offers no road to enduring peace, whatever the gains in territory.[15]

The lessons of the period between the Arab-Israeli conflicts in 1967 and in 1973 are that military occupation, even the most intelligent one, breeds humiliation and rebellion. Humiliation breeds sabotage. Sabotage breeds retaliation. Retaliation breeds terror. Terror breeds counterterror and thus another vicious circle is born.[16] Moreover, occupation of territories plants the seeds of future wars, as evidenced by the war of 1973.[17]

Based on their votes and statements in the late sixties, the overwhelming majority of the United Nations members were in agreement on the following basic points: (1) the United Nations Charter requires Israel to withdraw from all of the occupied Arab territories; (2) the state of belligerence between the Arabs and the Israelis must be ended; (3) all countries have the right to exist in peace and security and to enjoy innocent passage through international waterways; (4) the United Nations must play an active and essential role in dealing with the entire Middle East problem; and (5) only a just peace can be dependable and lasting.[18] These basic agreements compared favorably with the elements for a settlement which were acceptable to the United States and the Soviet Union and which were defined or implied in the famous Security Council Resolution 242. These elements include the following: withdrawal by Israel to the frontiers that existed on June 4, 1967, with slight rectifications in the Latrun area, including a strategic road connecting Tel Aviv with Jerusalem; some solution for Jerusalem which would satisfy both Israel's resolve to keep the city united under its control and the Arabs' resolve to maintain some sovereignty there; demilitarization of all returned territories; recognition by the Arabs of Israel's sovereignty and territorial integrity and the abolition of both the state of belligerency and the Arab boycott; free passage of Israeli ships through the Suez Canal and the Straits of Tiran; some compromise solution to the Palestinian refugee problem by returning lands to some and paying compensation to the others or by some combination of land and compensation; and international guarantees for the frontiers.[19]

With their occupation of Arab lands captured in 1967, Israel gained a political advantage in any future negotiations with the Arabs. Removal of this advantage might go a long way toward guaranteeing future peace in the Middle East, for as long as Israel maintains complete control of the occupied territories, the Arabs will not make peace with her.[20]

In addition, in order for peace to be a reality in the Middle East instead of there being merely a cease-fire, the Israelis must agree to abandon their expansionist policies and must begin to comply with modern, rather than with classical, international law—based, not on the illusion of omnipotence, but on what is feasible. Until Israel does this, the Arab-Israeli conflict will continue to exist as the Arab irresistible force colliding with the Israeli immovable object, and vice versa. As it now stands, the maximum offer of each side is less than the minimum acceptance of the other.[21] Thus, as former Secretary of State Dean Rusk has written, "there is merit in making it clear that the right of conquest must give way to the overriding requirement to maintain the peace and force cannot be used to acquire territory even where the use of force occurs under a claim of individual or collective self-defense."[22] Therefore, the international legal principle of the inadmissibility of the acquisition of territory by war demands Israeli withdrawal from the occupied territories whether Israel has the status of lawful occupant or of invader-occupant in those territories.

13

The Road to Peace and the Remaining Obstacles

When Neil Armstrong took his historic first step on the surface of the moon in July 1969, he said: "It's a small step for a man, but a giant leap for mankind." The treaty of peace signed by Israel and Egypt in Washington, D.C., March 26, 1979, was likewise a small step in the road to a just and lasting peace in the Middle East. Yet, it was also a giant leap for mankind in that it marked the first peace treaty of any sort between Israel and her Arab neighbors since her creation in 1948. The treaty of peace was the culmination of many agonizing efforts on the part of President Anwar Sadat of Egypt. Yet, that treaty was only the first step in a journey of a thousand miles.

On November 9, 1977, faced with news of more planned Israeli settlements in the West Bank of the occupied territories and faced with additional news of further Israeli attacks against Palestinian camps in south Lebanon, President Anwar Sadat of Egypt prepared to speak to his parliament. During the course of his speech, President Sadat proclaimed that he would go to Israel and speak to the Knesset itself in order to obtain peace in the Middle East.[1] Despite vehement disapproval throughout the Arab world of his plan to seek peace, and despite the resignation of his own foreign minister, President Sadat appeared before the Israeli Knesset—and before the world through the vehicle of television—and made a dramatic appeal for peace.[2] This appeal was followed by a series of talks between President Sadat, Israeli Prime Minister Menachem Begin, and their ministers. The talks were long and nonproductive, as the Israelis would agree only to withdrawal from Egyptian territory, as opposed to all of the Arab territory taken in the 1967 war.

President Jimmy Carter of the United States took it upon himself to act as mediator, and in the fall of 1978, he invited the two Middle Eastern leaders to the seclusion of Camp David, in the Maryland mountains, where all were kept in seclusion in an effort to reach a peace agreement. The Camp David Summit resulted in an agreement in principle for a peace treaty between the two nations, but not in substance—with the issue of the Palestinians still remaining an obstacle to the peace efforts. The question of Israeli settlements also remained a roadblock.[3] Yet the parties were realistic enough to know that a start in the peace process had to be made, and that start was made with the decision of the parties to agree to a treaty of peace between Egypt and Israel and to leave the Palestinian question for future negotiations. This chapter is intended to analyze the terms of the treaty of peace between Israel and Egypt and to examine the problems which the treaty deals with, as well as the problems which are not covered by the treaty.

The treaty of peace contains a preamble and nine articles. In addition, there is Annex I to the treaty, which contains nine articles; an appendix to Annex I, with eight articles; Annex II, with three maps depicting the Israeli withdrawal; Annex III, with eight articles; and Agreed Minutes to all of the articles. The preamble of the treaty makes the following points:

1. Both parties are convinced that there exists an urgent necessity for the establishment of a just, comprehensive, and lasting peace in the Middle East in accordance with Security Council Resolutions 242 and 338;
2. Both parties reaffirm their adherence to the "framework for peace in the Middle East agreed at Camp David" and signed September 17, 1978;
3. Both parties acknowledge that framework to be a basis for peace between all nations of the Middle East;

4. The parties desire to end the state of war between them and to establish a peace in which each state in the Middle East can live in security;
5. An Egyptian-Israeli peace is an important step in the search for a comprehensive peace in the Middle East;
6. Other Arab countries are invited to join the peace process with Israel;
7. The parties desire to develop friendly relations and cooperation in accordance with the United Nations Charter and principles of international law in time of peace;
8. The parties agree to the nine articles of the treaty in the free exercise of their sovereignty in order to implement the framework for peace between the two parties;[4]

The preamble is intended to outline the general purpose of the agreement between the parties and is valuable in interpreting the agreement. In this case, Egypt and Israel both agree that peace in the Middle East *must* be in accordance with Security Council Resolutions 242 and 338 in order to be just and lasting. Resolution 338 ordered the cease fire in the Yom Kippur War in 1973 and reaffirmed the principles of Resolution 242. Resolution 242 is the premise behind the United Nations demand that Israel withdraw from the lands taken during the 1967 war; it declares the inadmissibility of the taking of those lands by conquest, or in other words, it forbids the conquest of lands in and / or by war by refusing to recognize the legality of such conquests, in the hope that the land taken will eventually be returned. By signing the treaty, Israel has agreed to the principle set forth in Resolution 242.

The preamble likewise outlines the fact that this treaty is only part of the solution to the problems of the Middle East and that other steps must be taken in order to implement a comprehensive, just, and lasting peace. The framework for such a peace was outlined in the Camp David Accords of September 17, 1978. At the same time, the preamble adopts the Israeli position that each country is entitled to be secure behind its borders and thus quashes the hard-line Palestinian concept of driving the Israelis back into the sea, from whence they came. The parties to the treaty further invite the participation of other Arab countries in the peacemaking process and show the desire of those parties to establish friendship and cooperation in accordance with peacetime principles of international law.

Article I provides for the following items:

1. The parties will terminate the state of war between them and will establish a condition of peace once the treaty has been ratified by each country;
2. Israel will withdraw *all* of its armed forces *and civilians* from the Sinai behind the international boundary, as outlined in Annex I;
3. Egypt will resume the exercise of its full sovereignty over the Sinai;
4. Once withdrawal is completed for the interim period, the parties will establish full diplomatic relations.

This article establishes the termination of the state of war between Egypt and Israel and the establishment of the long-sought peace. At the same time, there exists a potential problem regarding the withdrawal provision. The article requires the withdrawal of both military and civilian personnel. Political realities come into play at this juncture. During the twelve years of occupation of the Sinai, Israeli settlements have been established—some of the settlements being military or quasi-military in nature and others being purely civilian. Does this provision require all Israeli citizens to leave the Sinai? Such an interpretation is realistic. During the negotiations for the treaty, news reports brought out the questions in the minds of the Israeli citizens living and working on the Sinai peninsula. If full military and civilian withdrawal is achieved, then a great victory will have been attained and Resolution 242 will have been fully implemented as far as the Egyptians are concerned.

Article II is brief but highly important, as it sets out the boundaries of the two nations. The article provides that:

1. The permanent boundary between Egypt and Israel is the international boundary as shown on the map of Annex II;

2. The issue of the status of the Gaza Strip is not covered by this treaty and is open for future negotiations;
3. Each party agrees to respect the territorial integrity of the other including territorial waters and airspace.[5]

Article II provides for the first exception or exemption from coverage, that being the Gaza Strip. The article also provides for the inviolability of the territory of each country, including territorial waters and airspace.

Article III outlines the guidelines for the manner in which the two nations will act toward each other in the international community. Article III states:

1. The parties will abide by the Charter of the United Nations and principles of international law in times of peace;
2. The parties will recognize each other's right to sovereignty, territorial integrity, and political independence;
3. The parties acknowledge the right of each to live in peace within secure and recognized boundaries;
4. Each party will not threaten or use force against the other party and will settle all disputes by peaceful means;
5. Each party will insure that acts or threats of violence do not originate from or are not committed by forces subject to its control, or any other forces stationed in its territory, against the population, citizens, or property of the other party;
6. Each party will refrain from instigating, inciting, assisting, or participating in acts of violence and insures that if persons are involved in acts of violence against the other party and if such persons are within the boundaries of the party, such party will bring the violent actors or perpetrators to justice;
7. Each party will accord to the other full diplomatic recognition, including diplomatic and cultural services;
8. Each party will terminate existing economic boycotts and barriers which preclude the free movement of goods and / or people;
9. Annex III outlines the method by which such relationships are to be established.[6]

Article III is written in "traditional legalese," language which will be better understood by international lawyers than by the citizens of the countries involved. Initially, the parties agree to abide by the Charter of the United Nations, and they also agree to follow the general principles of international law. Each party acknowledges the right of the other to "do their own thing" inside of their own borders. The term "secure and recognized borders" is not nebulous this time, as the borders are defined as those between Egypt and Israel. The question of "recognized borders" does remain, however, with respect to the other occupied territories, in that Resolution 242 does not recognize Israel's rights to any of the lands taken during the 1967 war.

Article III goes on to provide for the peaceful resolution of disputes between Egypt and Israel. Political realities dictate that disputes will occur in the future. Rather than go to war over the disputes, the parties agree to settle such disputes by peaceful means. Article VII outlines that should a dispute occur, the parties will attempt to negotiate a solution. Should the negotiators fail to come to some sort of agreement, the parties agree to submit the issue to arbitration. Numerous forums exist for the settling of such disputes, including the submission of those disputes to the International Court of Justice at The Hague.

Another provision of Article III requires each party to make certain that none of its soldiers or civilians commits acts of violence against the other party. At the same time, one party can allow a belligerent third party to attack the other party from stations within its own borders. The classic example of a situation such as that described is the Palestinian terrorists who operate from southern Lebanon. According to the terms of the treaty, each party is obligated to prevent such acts from taking place. In the unfortunate event that such an act occurs, each party is obligated to "bring the perpetrator to Justice."

Finally, Article III accords full diplomatic and consular services to each party, requiring each party to take down any barriers which might hamper the free movement of people or goods between countries. It also acknowledges that the method for setting up full diplomatic services is outlined in Annex III.

It is interesting to note that although the treaty attempts to deal with the problems the Israelis have encountered with the PLO in southern Lebanon, the treaty has no effect in terms of political realities on the PLO. At the same time, the treaty does prohibit either party from assisting or participating in acts of violence against the other party. This may or may not have any effect on terrorist activities, depending upon the definition of *assisting*. Nowhere have there been any allegations that Egypt ever "assisted" the PLO in any terrorist activity in the past. Such activities seem to come regularly from the PLO without any assistance whatsoever. Once again a conflict becomes apparent between international law and political realities.

Article IV provides for United Nations observers, as well as a joint commission to implement the provisions, particularly the withdrawal portions of the treaty. In addition, the treaty provides for the permanent stationing of United Nations personnel in the areas described in Annex I. In that way, there will be some way of insuring that the peace will be kept, and border flare-ups can be prevented.

Article V designates the Straits of Tiran and the Gulf of Aqaba as international waterways, thereby precluding the sort of blockade that inevitably led to the 1967 war. At the same time, Israeli ships are guaranteed the right of free passage through the Suez Canal, the Gulf of Suez, and the Mediterranean Sea under the Constantinople Convention of 1888.

Political realities surrounding Article VI nearly precluded agreement on the treaty, as the question arose of Egypt's obligations to other Arab countries, which are still hostile to Israel, and whether or not Egypt would be able to go to war, or to support other Arab countries should hostilities erupt between Israel and other Arab countries. Article VI provides that

1. The treaty does not affect the rights and obligations of the parties under the Charter of the United Nations;
2. The parties will fulfill their obligations under this treaty in good faith without regard to any prior treaties with any other parties;

3. Each party will notify the secretary-general of the United Nations as to what other multilateral treaties they are parties to and shall notify the other parties as to the obligations of this treaty;
4. Neither party will enter into any future agreement with any nation which conflicts with any of the terms and / or provisions of this treaty;
5. This treaty will be controlling over any prior treaty and / or obligation which conflicts with the treaty.[7]

Hence, the treaty is clear in stating that its terms and provisions supersede any other treaty commitment by either party. That section is most important to Israel in light of prior Arab solidarity. At the same time, there is a notice requirement, stating that the parties must notify the secretary-general of the United Nations of multilateral treaty commitments and thereby give the secretary-general an opportunity to determine whether or not there will be any future conflicts between treaty obligations.

Article VIII establishes a claims commission for the mutual settlement of all financial claims. Here again, the question of political realities comes into play. For example, if Israel citizens have to leave their homes and businesses in the Sinai in order to comply with the terms of withdrawal, will they have redress from the commission for their claims? What claims will be honored? What about the claims of Egyptian landowners who lost their lands and / or business due to the Israeli occupation?

The importance of Article IX is that it makes the English text prevail if a dispute arises over the translation of the Hebrew and Arabic versions. At the same time, despite the importance of the Camp David Accords of September 1978, the treaty provides that the treaty itself is the final agreement between the parties.

In order to properly interpret the treaty, one must examine the annexes to it, as they provide the specific details missing in the body of the treaty itself. Annex I is entitled "Protocol Concerning Israeli Withdrawal and Security Arrangements." Among its provisions are the following:

1. Complete withdrawal of Israeli armed forces and civilians shall take place not later than three years from the date of ratification of the treaty by the two countries;
2. The first phase of withdrawal shall take place within nine months of ratification;
3. A joint commission will supervise and coordinate the withdrawal;
4. Details of the commission are set forth in Article IV of the appendix, and the commission will be dissolved upon completion of the withdrawal;
5. The Egyptian armed forces which will take over the military installations and field fortifications are described;
6. Provisions are made for entry only by checkpoints designated by each party;
7. The type of air activity permitted on the airfield is described;
8. Naval activities permitted in the areas are described;
9. Limitations are placed on the operation of early-warning systems;
10. United Nations operations are described.

Annex I provides many of the details for the practical management of the military installations which are on the Sinai, so that no misunderstanding will come about as to whether or not a military buildup is or is not taking place in violation of the terms of the treaty.

Specifics for the Israeli withdrawal itself are covered by the appendix to Annex I, which is entitled "Organization of Movements in the Sinai." Article II outlines each subphase of withdrawal and the deployment of Egyptian forces. Article III emphasizes that the United Nations forces will employ their best efforts to supervise the withdrawal and to prevent any violation of the terms and provisions for withdrawal.

As indicated above, Article IV sets up the joint commission to supervise the withdrawal. Certain factors concerning this joint commission are worth noting:

1. The commission shall be comprised of senior officers of each party;
2. The commission can call a representative of the United Nations to be present during meetings;
3. All decisions must be made by the consensus of the parties;
4. The commission shall coordinate military movements and resolve any problems;
5. It will submit any problem which cannot be resolved to the respective governments of Egypt and Israel for resolution in accordance with the terms of the treaty;
6. It will organize the demarcation of boundary lines;
7. It will supervise the handing over of main installations from Israel to Egypt;
8. It will agree on necessary arrangements for the finding and returning of missing bodies of Egyptian and Israeli soldiers;
9. It will organize and operate entry checkpoints;
10. It will conduct its operations through the use of liaison teams consisting of one Israeli and one Egyptian;
11. It will coordinate United Nations forces and / or monitors;
12. The joint commission shall meet monthly, and special meetings can be called within twenty-four hours;
13. The first meeting of the commission shall take place within two weeks of the entry into force of the treaty.

Article IV goes into explicit detail as to the operations and purpose of the joint commission. The practical success of the transition of the Sinai back to Egypt depends upon the ability of the joint commission to conduct its operations effectively. At the same time, the members of the commission, and in particular the members of the liaison group will have to work together effectively in order to guarantee the success of the transition. The commission and its operations are well thought out, and its tasks and limitations are well defined. With an efficient joint commission, the transition of the Sinai and the treaty itself should operate smoothly.

Article V outlines the operations of the various parties and the United Nations forces in the buffer zones, including limitations on the type of weaponry which can be carried into the buffer zones. Article VI permits technical teams from Egypt to learn from Israeli technicians the operations and / or the structures of the installations being transferred to Egypt. It also requires the Israelis to remove all military barriers and / or mine fields near such installations. Article VII governs surveillance activities, while Article VIII allows for the resumption of Egyptian sovereignty.

Annex III outlines the protocol which is to be used in the establishment of diplomatic and economic relations between Egypt and Israel. The terms of this section are clear and straightforward, requiring the establishment of diplomatic, consular, trade, and cultural relations. Article IV provides for the freedom of movement of persons and goods between the two nations in accordance with the privileges extended to persons and goods of other nations. Article V provides for development of good and friendly relations. Article VI is the only "technical" section in Annex III, as it deals with transportation and telecommunications. The article provides that the airfields being taken over by the Egyptians shall only be used for civil aviation and shall be open for commercial use by all nations. At the same time, the parties shall maintain roads and railroads between the two nations and shall comply with existing international conventions and regulations regarding communication and postal services.

Article VII can only be attributed to President Jimmy Carter, whose quest for human rights has become a mainstay of American foreign policy during his term as president. Finally, Article VIII reiterates the right of innocent passage through territorial seas, which is an important principle of international law.

This treaty of peace between Egypt and Israel becomes international law between the two nations. However, two important points should be noted. The first point is that one of the major stumbling blocks to peace in the Middle East is the establishment of Israeli settlements in the occupied territories. The treaty is silent on that issue. United Nations Security Council Resolution 242 prohibits the acquisition of territory by force by refusing to recognize such acquisition. That problem remains for future negotiations. The second problem is the Palestinians and their right to a homeland. The treaty is silent on that issue as well. The United Nations resolutions acknowledge the rights of the Palestinians as a quasi-state. Yet that problem, too, remains for future negotiations.

It is said that a journey of a thousand miles begins with a single step. However, that step alone does not get one to his thousand-mile destination. In the case of the Middle East, some start had to be made in order to expect to attain the goal of a comprehensive and just peace. That first step came with the journey of Anwar Sadat to Israel. The next important step came with the Camp David Accords. Those efforts culminated with the treaty of peace between Egypt and Israel. Yet, that peace treaty is not an end in itself, only another beginning. The end will not come until the problem of the Palestinians in the occupied Arab territories has been solved. The vehicle for the solution of the Palestinian problem is Security Council Resolution 242. The roadblocks to a successful implementation of Resolution 242 are the continued Israeli occupation of the territories taken in the 1967 war and the continuing policy of increasing the number of Jewish settlements on those occupied territories. Yet if other Arab countries would accept Resolution 242 and recognize the state of Israel at its 1967 borders rather than strive to dismantle the state of Israel or to "drive them into the sea" perhaps the Egyptian-Israeli treaty of peace could be expanded and Resolution 242 fully implemented.

International law provides a vehicle for the resolution of the Middle East situation, including the problems of the Palestinians. Political realities on both sides, Arab and Israeli, preclude effective solution and maintain a volatile state of affairs in the region.

Notes

1. INTERNATIONAL LAW AND CONFLICT RESOLUTION

1. Quoted in Martin W. Kronish, *Letter to the Editor,* New York Times, Oct. 24, 1973, p. 42. (Mr. Kronish is currently treasurer of the World Federalists.)

2. Quoted in Mohammed H. El-Zayyat, *The Situation in the Middle East* (pamphlet), p. 2.

3. Israel listed six very broad reservations, while Egypt limited compulsory jurisdiction solely to disputes arising as to use of the Suez Canal under the Constantinople Convention of 1888; see Howard Golden, *International Legal Solutions to the Middle East Crisis,* 6 The International Lawyer 506 (July 1972).

4. Roger Fisher, *Dear Israelis, Dear Arabs,* p. 10. (Mr. Fisher is a professor of International Law at Harvard.)

5. Isaac Shapiro, "Introduction," to Quincy Wright, The *Middle East: Prospects for Peace,* p. x.

6. John W. Halderman, *Symposium: The Middle East Crisis,* 33 Law and Contemporary Problems 44 (winter 1968).

2. THE ONE-SIDED PERSPECTIVE

1. Arie Bober, ed., *The Other Israel,* p. 260.

2. Michael W. Suleiman, in *The Arab-Israeli Confrontation of June 1967: An Arab Perspective,* ed. Ibrahim Abu-Lughod, p. 138.

3. M. Charif Bassiouni, *The Middle East: The Misunderstood Conflict,* 19 Kansas Law Review 394 (1971).

4. Suleiman, in *Arab-Israeli Confrontation,* ed. Abu-Lughod, pp. 139, 143-44, 147.

5. Malcolm H. Kerr, "Foreword," in *Arab-Israeli Confrontation,* ed. Abu-Lughod, p. vii.

6. Suleiman, *supra* note 4, at 141.
7. Kerr, *supra* note 7, at vii-viii.
8. Quoted in Suleiman, *supra* note 4, at 139.
9. Kerr, *supra* note 7.
10. Maxine Rodinson, "Foreword" to David Waines, *The Unholy War*, p. 11.
11. Quoted from British Broadcasting Monitaring Service, *Summary of World Broadcasts: Part 4—The Middle East and Africa,* Jan. 22, 1973, p. A / 1.
12. Dr. Karnel S. Abu-Jaber, in *Arab-Israeli Confrontation,* ed. Abu-Lughod, p. 167.

3. WHY IS IT IMPORTANT WHO STARTED THE 1967 WAR?

1. I. L. Kenen et al., *A Just Peace in the Middle East: How Can It Be Achieved?* p. 22.
2. Myron S. Kaufmann, *The Coming Destruction of Israel,* pp. 57-58.
3. *Id.*
4. Allen Gerson, *Trustee-Occupant: The Legal Status of Israel's Presence in the West Bank,* 14 Harvard International Law Journal 6 (1973).
5. Julius Stone, *Legal Controls of International Conflict,* p. 694.
6. Quoted in Gerson, *supra* note 4, at 4-5.
7. *Id.* at 5.

4. WHO REALLY STARTED THE 1967 WAR? A LOOK AT BOTH SIDES

1. Amos Shapira, *The Six-Day War and the Right of Self Defense,* 6 Israel Law Review 68 (1971). (Mr. Shapira has his S.J.D. from Yale University and is a lecturer at Tel Aviv University.)
2. M. Charif Bassiouni, *The Middle East: The Misunderstood Conflict,* 19 Kansas Law Review 394 (1971).
3. Allen Gerson, *Trustee-Occupant: The Legal Status of Israel's Presence in the West Bank,* 14 Harvard International Law Journal 18 (1973).
4. *Id.* at 19-20.
5. Quoted in Mohammed H. El-Zayyat, *The Situation in the Middle East,* p. 25. n. 5.

6. Bassiouni, *supra* note 2, at 395.
7. El-Zayyat, *supra* note 5.
8. William V. O'Brien, *International Law and the Outbreak of War in the Middle East,* 11 Orbis 720 fall (1967).
9. Bassiouni, *supra* note 2, at 395.
10. O'Brien, *supra* note 8, at 717.
11. Abdul-Hafez M. Elkordy, *Crisis of Diplomacy,* pp. 152-53.
12. American Friends Service Committee, *The Search for Peace in the Middle East,* p. 35.
13. Hisham Sharabi in *The Arab-Israeli Confrontation of June 1967,* ed. Ibrahim Abu-Lughod, p. 52.
14. El-Zayyat, *supra* note 5, at 24 n. 5.
15. Amos Shapira, *The Security Council Resolution of November 22, 1967: Its Legal Nature and Implications,* 4 Israel Law Review 236 (1969).
16. Bassiouni, *supra* note 2, at 395.
17. Sharabi, *supra* note 13, at 56-57.
18. Quoted in Donald C. Piper, *The Legal Control of the Use of Force and the Definition of Aggression,* 2 Georgia Journal of International and Comparative Law 11 (1972).
19. *Id.* at 3-4.
20. Karnel S. Abu-Jaber, in *Arab-Israeli Confrontation of June 1967,* ed. Abu-Lughod, p. 157. (Mr. Abu-Jaber is professor of government at Smith College.)
21. David Waines, *The Unholy War,* p. 162. (Mr. Waines is a member of the faculty at the Institute of Islamic Studies, McGill University.)
22. Abu-Jaber, *supra* note 20.
23. Sharabi, *supra* note 13.
24. *Id.* at 169 n. 1.
25. Abu-Lughod, *supra* note 13, at 89-90.
26. Quoted in El-Zayyat, *supra* note 5, at 25 n. 5.
27. Quoted in Sharabi, *supra* note 13, at 54-55.
28. Bassiouni, *supra* note 2, at 395.
29. 10 United Nations Monthly Chronicle 41 (July 1973).
30. Quoted in El-Zayyat, *supra* note 5, at 11.
31. *Id.*
32. John Lawrence Hargrove, *Abating the Middle East Crisis through the United Nations (and Vice Versa),* 19 Kansas Law Review 366-67 (1971).
33. Bassiouni, *supra* note 2, at 395.
34. Julius Stone, *The November Resolution and Middle East Peace: Pitfall or Guidepost,* 1971 University of Toledo Law Review 56.

5. SECURITY COUNCIL RESOLUTION 242 AND INTERNATIONAL LAW

1. Allen Pollack, in I. L. Kenen et al., *A Just Peace in the Mideast: How Can It Be Achieved?* p. 73.
2. 10 United Nations Monthly Chronicle 5 (July 1973).
3. Uri Avnery, in *The Third Year of the Six Days War: Reflections on the Middle East Crisis,* ed. Herbert Mason, p. 162.
4. Quincy Wright, *The Middle East Problem,* 64 American Journal of International Law 270 (1970).
5. C. H. Dodd and M. E. Sales, *Israel and the Arab World,* p. 111.
6. Julius Stone, *The November Resolution and Middle East Peace: Pitfall or Guidepost,* 1971 University of Toledo Law Review 47.
7. Carnegie Endowment for International Peace, *Issues before the 25th General Assembly,* 1970 International Conciliation 14.
8. Dodd and Sales, *supra* note 5, at 185.
9. Josef Tekoah, *Statement before the Security Council,* 10 United Nations Monthly Chronicle 27 (July 1973).
10. Abdul-Hafez M. Elkordy, *Crisis of Diplomacy,* p. 217.
11. Tekoah, *supra* note 9, at 10.
12. Mohammed H. El-Zayyat, *Statement before the Security Council,* 10 United Nations Monthly Chronicle 21 (1973).
13. David Waines, *The Unholy War,* p. 152.
14. Abdulla El-Erian, in Quincy Wright, *The Middle East: Prospects for Peace,* ed. Isaac Shapiro, p. 66.
15. Mohammed H. El-Zayyat, *Statement before the Security Council,* 9 United Nations Monthly Chronicle 96 (June 1972).
16. El-Zayyat, *supra* note 12.
17. Elias Sam'o and Cyrus Elahi, *Resolution 242 and Beyond,* The Arab World, August-September 1971, p. 32.
18. American Friends Service Committee, *Search for Peace in the Middle East,* p. 80.
19. Quoted in Tekoah, *supra* note 9, at 27.
20. E. Dmitriyev, *Middle East: Dangerous Tension Must Go,* International Affairs (Moscow) July 7, 1973, p. 30.
21. John Scali, *Statement before the United Nations General Assembly,* 69 Department of State Bulletin 271 (Aug. 20, 1973).
22. *Id.* at 270.
23. Mohammed H. El-Zayyat, *The Situation in the Middle East,* p. 18 n. 2.
24. Wright, *supra* note 4.
25. *Id.*

26. Yakov Malik, *Statement before the Security Council,* 10 United Nations Monthly Chronicle 33 (July 1973). (Mr. Malik was the Soviet Union's representative to the United Nations.)

27. El-Zayyat, *supra* note 23, at 18 n. 5.

28. Quoted *id.* at 28 n. 18.

29. U.N. Doc A/RES/2625 (xxv, 1970).

30. Wright, *supra* note 4, at 271.

31. *Id.*

32. Elkordy, *supra* note 10, at 201-3.

33. Quoted in Elmer Berger, in I. L. Kenen et al., *A Just Peace in the Middle East: How Can It Be Achieved?* 55 (1971).

34. *Id.*

35. *U.S. News and World Report,* Oct. 29, 1973, p. 21; Christopher Mayhew, *A Just Peace in the Middle East: How Can It Be Achieved?* p. 111.

36. Myron S. Kaufmann, *The Coming Destruction of Israel,* pp. 57-58.

37. John Norton Moore, *The Arab-Israeli Conflict and the Obligation to Pursue Peaceful Settlement of International Disputes,* 19 Kansas Law Review 426 (1971).

38. Dr. Yoram Dinstein, *The Arab-Israeli Crisis: Legal Issues and Possible Solutions,* 4 The International Lawyer (1970).

39. *Hearings on the Middle East Conflict before the Subcomm. on the Near East of the House Comm. on Foreign Affairs,* 92nd Cong., 1st Sess. 196 (1971).

40. Stone, *supra* note 6, at 59.

41. M. Charif Bassiouni, *The Middle East in Transition,* 4 The International Lawyer 383 (1970).

42. Nathan Feinburg, *The Arab-Israeli Conflict in International Law,* p. 118.

43. John Lawrence Hargrove, *Abating the Middle East Crisis through the United Nations (and Vice Versa),* 19 University of Kansas Law Review 367 (1971).

44. Wright, *supra* note 4, at 271.

45. Elkordy, *supra* note 10, at 140.

46. Robert D. Kamenshire, *Peacekeeping and Peacemaking—The United Nations in the Middle East,* 1 The Vanderbilt International 14 (winter-spring 1967-68).

47. Elkordy, *supra* note 10, at 140.

48. Muhammad H. El-Farra, *The Role of the United Nations vis-à-vis the Palestine Question,* 33 Law and Contemporary Problems 75 (1968).

49. Kamenshire, *supra* note 46.

55. British Broadcasting Monitoring Service, *Summary of World Broadcasts: Part 4—The Middle East and Africa,* Feb. 6, 1973, p. A / 1.

56. Israeli Ministry for Foreign Affairs, *supra* note 31.

57. Waines, *supra* note 5, at 158-59.

58. Teveth, *supra* note 25, at 268, 270.

59. Dib and Jabber, *supra* note 4, at xxxiv.

60. *Facts on File 1971,* Jan. 1-6, 1971, pp. 9-10.

61. El-Zayyat, *supra* note 26, at 26 n. 6.

62. Waines, *supra* note 5, at 162.

63. Roger Fisher, in *The Arab-Israeli Confrontation of June 1967,* ed. Ibrahim Abu-Lughod, p. 167.

64. Fred J. Khouri, *The Arab-Israeli Dilemma,* pp. 332-33.

65. Quoted in Dib and Jabber, *supra* note 4, at 196.

66. *Id.* at 192.

67. Muhammad H. El-Farra, *The Role of the United Nations vis-à-vis the Palestine Question,* 33 Law and Contemporary Problems 75 (1968).

7. ISRAEL'S SECURITY AND THE QUESTION OF BORDERS

1. Quoted in Adman Al-Pachachi, *Statement before the Security Council,* 10 United Nations Monthly Chronicle 41 (July 1973). (Mr. Al-Pachachi is the foreign minister for the United Arab Emirates.)

2. Quoted in George Dib and Faud Jabber, *Israel's Violation of Human Rights in the Occupied Territories,* p. 209.

3. Christopher Mayhew, in I. L. Kenen et al., *A Just Peace in the Middle East: How Can It Be Achieved?* p. 115.

4. Israeli Ministry for Foreign Affairs, *The Meaning of "Secure Borders,"* p. 1.

5. Kamel S. Abu-Jaber, in *The Arab-Israeli Confrontation of June 1967,* ed. Ibrahim Abu-Lughod, 1970, 160-61.

6. Yosef Tekoah, *Statement before the Security Council,* 10 United Nations Monthly Chronicle 18 (July 1973).

7. Roger Fisher, *Dear Israelis, Dear Arabs,* p. 36.

8. Washington Post, Oct. 10, 1973, § A, p. 15.

9. Tekoah, *supra* note 6, at 28.

10. Roger Fisher, in *The Arab-Israeli Confrontation of June 1967,* ed. Ibrahim Abu-Lughod, p. 167.

11. John Norton Moore, *The Arab-Israeli Conflict and the Obligation to Pursue Peaceful Settlement of International Disputes,* 19 University of Kansas Law Review 425 (1971).

12. Don Peretz, *Israel's Administration and Arab Refugees,* 46 Foreign Affairs 339 (1968).
13. Myron S. Kaufmann, *The Coming Destruction of Israel,* pp. 61-62.
14. Abdul-Hafez M. Elkordy, *Crisis of Diplomacy,* p. 217.
15. Tekoah, *supra* note 6, at 30.
16. Kaufmann, *supra* note 13, at 58.
17. Earmot Abdul Meguid, *Statement before the Security Council,* 10 United Nations Monthly Chronicle 29 (July 1973).
18. 10 United Nations Monthly Chronicle 49 (July 1973).
19. Louis de Guiringaud, *Statement before the Security Council,* 10 United Nations Monthly Chronicle 40 (July 1973).
20. Moore, *supra* note 11, at 426.
21. John Lawrence Hargrove, *Abating the Middle East Crisis through the United Nations (and Vice Versa),* 19 Kansas Law Review 371 (1971).
22. *Hearings on the Middle East Conflict before the Subcomm. on the Near East of the House Comm. on Foreign Affairs,* 92nd Cong., 1st Sess. 196 (1971).
23. Quoted in Elias Sam'o and Cyrus Elahi, *Resolution 242 and Beyond,* The Arab World, Aug / Sept, 1971, p. 33.
24. Mayhew, *supra* note 3, at 111, Maxine Rodinson, *Israel and the Arabs,* p. 228.
25. U.S. News & World Report, Oct. 29, 1973, at 21.
26. Mayhew, *supra* note 3, at 115-16.
27. *Id.*
28. Quoted in Sam'o and Elahi, *supra* note 23, at 35.
29. David Waines, *The Unholy War,* pp. 152, 165.
30. Israeli Ministry for Foreign Affairs, *supra* note 4, at 14.
31. Sam'o and Elahi, *supra* note 23, at 33.
32. Al-Pachachi, *supra* note 1.
33. Waines, *supra* note 29, at 154.
34. Michael W. Suleiman in *The Arab-Israeli Confrontation of June 1967,* ed. Ibrahim Abu-Lughod, p. 147.
35. Mayhew, *supra* note 3, at 150, 115.
36. Mohammed H. El-Zayyat, *The Situation in the Middle East,* p. 6.
37. Mayhew, *supra* note 3, at 115.
38. Hisham Sharabi, in *The Arab-Israeli Confrontation of June 1967,* ed. Ibrahim Abu-Lughod, p. 98.
39. Waines, *supra* note 29, at 158.
40. Sharabi, *supra* note 38.
41. Quoted in Dib and Jabber, *supra* note 2, at 196.
42. Mayhew, *supra* note 3, at 116.

43. El-Zayyat, *supra* note 36, at 26 n. 6.
44. Quoted in Dib and Jabber, *supra* note 2, at 215.
45. Arie Bober, ed., *The Other Israel,* p. 277.
46. Waines, *supra* note 29, at 155.
47. El-Zayyat, *supra* note 36, at 18 n. 2.
48. *Id.* at 22 n. 18.
49. Quoted in *Newsweek,* March 29, 1971, p. 37.

8. A CRITICAL LOOK AT ISRAELI ARGUMENTS

1. Quincy Wright, *The Middle East: Prospects for Peace,* ed. Isaac Shapiro, pp. 55, 67.
2. Mohammed H. El-Zayyat, *The Situation in the Middle East,* p. 12.
3. Quoted in Ralph H. Magnus, ed., *Documents on the Middle East,* p. 171.
4. El-Zayyat, *supra* note 2, at 2, 17.
5. Yosef Tekoah, *Statement before the Security Council,* 10 United Nations Monthly Chronicle 21 (July 1973).
6. Maxine Rodinson, *Israel and the Arabs,* p. 228.
7. El-Zayyat, *supra* note 2, at 11.
8. Quincy Wright, *The Middle East Problem,* 64 Journal of International Law 270 (1970).
9. John Lawrence Hargrove, *Abating the Middle East Crisis through the United Nations (and Vice Versa),* 19 Kansas Law Review 367 (1971).
10. Esmat Abdul Meguid, *Statement before the Security Council,* 10 United Nations Monthly Chronicle 29 (July 1973).
11. Myron S. Kaufmann, *The Coming Destruction of Israel,* pp. 57-58.
12. Hargrove, *supra* note 9, at 367 n. 1.
13. M. Charif Bassiouni, *The Middle East: The Misunderstood Conflict,* 19 Kansas Law Review 394 (1971).
14. Allen Gerson, *Trustee-Occupant: The Legal Status of Israel's Presence in the West Bank,* 14 Harvard International Law Journal 40 (1973).
15. David Waines, *The Unholy War,* pp. 16, 162.
16. El-Zayyat, *supra* note 2, at 4.
17. Shabtai Rosenne, *Directions for a Middle East Settlement,* 33 Law and Contemporary Problems 44 n. 1 (1968).
18. Rodinson, *supra* note 6, at 230.
19. 8 United Nations Monthly Chronicle 3 (Feb. 1971).
20. El-Zayyat, supra note 2, at 4.

21. Roger Fisher in *The Arab-Israeli Confrontation of June 1967*, ed. Ibrahim Abu-Lughod, p. 164.
22. El-Zayyat, *supra* note 2, at 21 n. 16.
23. *Id.* at 25 n. 5.
24. Gerson, *supra* note 14, at 15, 8.
25. Julius Stone, *Legal Controls of International Conflict*, p. 694.
26. *Facts on File 1971*, Dec. 9-15, 1971, p. 965.

9. THE ARAB PERCEPTION OF THE MIDDLE EAST CRISIS

1. Christopher Mayhew in I. L. Kenen et al., *A Just Peace in the Middle East: How Can It Be Achieved?* p. 111.
2. Kamel S. Abu-Jaber in *The Arab-Israeli Confrontation of June 1967*, ed. Ibrahim Abu-Lughod, p. 156.
3. Mohammed H. El-Zayyat, *The Situation in the Middle East*, p. 11.
4. Elmer Berger in I. L. Kenen et al., *A Just Peace in the Middle East: How Can It Be Achieved?* pp. 61-62.
5. Quoted in *Facts on File 1971*, March 11-17, 1971, at 181.
6. Quoted in George Dib and Faud Jabber, *Israel's Violation of Human Rights in the Occupied Territories*, p. 215.
7. *Id.*
8. *Hearings on Approaches to Peace in the Middle East before the Subcomm. on the Near East of the House Comm. on Foreign Affairs*, 92nd Cong., 2nd Sess. 35 (1972).
9. El-Zayyat, *supra* note 3, at 6.
10. *Id.* at 4.
11. Mohammed H. El-Zayyat, *Statement before the Security Council*, 10 United Nations Monthly Chronicle 7 (July 1973).
12. Quoted in David Waines, *The Unholy War*, p. 153.
13. El-Zayyat, *supra* note 3, at 18 n. 8.
14. Uri Avnery, *The Third Year of the Six Days War*, in *Reflections on the Middle East Crisis*, ed. Herbert Mason, p. 155.
15. Roger Fisher in *The Arab-Israeli Confrontation of June 1967*, ed. Ibrahim Abu-Lughod, p. 164.
16. El-Zayyat, *supra* note 3, at 14.
17. Carnegie Endowment for International Peace, *Issues before the 26th General Assembly*, 1971 International Conciliation no. 584, at 36.
18. Mayhew, *supra* note 1, at 112-13.
19. *Id.* at 116.
20. Dib and Jabber, *supra* note 6, at 213.

21. El-Zayyat, *supra* note 3, at 4.
22. El-Zayyat, *supra* note 3, at 14.
23. Fisher, *supra* note 15, at 161.
24. El-Zayyat, *supra* note 3, at 20 n. 13, p. 6.
25. Quincy Wright, *The Middle East: Prospects for Peace,* ed. Isaac Shapiro, p. 80.
26. El-Zayyat, *supra* note 3, at 12.
27. Shapiro, *supra* note 27, at 67.
28. American Friends Service Committee, *The Search for Peace in the Middle East,* p. 80.
29. Berger, *supra* note 4, at 56.
30. Quoted in *New York Times,* Oct. 12, 1973, p. 19.
31. El-Zayyat, *supra* note 3, at 17.
32. *Id.* at 24 n. 3.
33. *Id.* at 26 n. 9.
34. *Id.* at 8, 10.

10. THE EVER-CHANGING UNITED STATES POSITION ON THE MIDDLE EAST

1. Quincy Wright, *The Middle East Problem,* 64 American Journal of International Law 271 (1970).
2. Kamel S. Abu-Jaber in *The Arab-Israeli Confrontation of June 1967,* ed. Ibrahim Abu-Lughod, pp. 160-61, 157.
3. Quoted in Adman Al-Pachachi, *Statement before the Security Council,* 10 United Nations Monthly Chronicle 41 (July 1973).
4. John Lawrence Hargrove, *Abating the Middle East Crisis through the United Nations (and Vice Versa),* 19 Kansas Law Review 368 (1971).
5. Wright, *supra* note 1, at 272.
6. Mohammed H. El-Zayyat, *The Situation in the Middle East,* p. 22 n. 18.
7. Christopher Mayhew in I. L. Kenen et al., *A Just Peace in the Middle East: How Can It Be Achieved?* pp. 124-25.
8. John Scali, *Statement before the General Assembly,* 69 Department of State Bulletin 271 (Aug. 20, 1973).
9. I. L. Kenen et al., *A Just Peace in the Middle East: How Can It Be Achieved?* pp. 18-19.
10. Elmer Berger in I. L. Kenen et al., *A Just Peace in the Middle East: How Can It Be Achieved?* pp. 65-66.

11. THE YOM KIPPUR WAR–1973

1. See British Broadcasting Company, *Summary of World Broadcasts: Part 4—The Middle East and Africa,* Oct. 8, 1973.
2. *Keesing's Contemporary Archives,* Nov. 5-11, 1973, p. 26173.
3. *Id.*
4. *Id.* at 26197.
5. *Id.* at 26198, 26199.
6. *Id.* at 26176.
7. *Id.* at 26197.
8. M. Adams, *The Arab-Israeli Confrontation, 1967-78,* in *The Middle East and North Africa (1977-78),* p. 36.
9. *Id.* at 52.
10. *Id.* at 36.
11. *Id.* at 53.
12. D. Dishon, *Middle East Record,* 4 (1968) 445, 453.
13. *Id.* at 456.
14. M. Adams, *supra* note 8, at 37.
15. *Id.* at 41.
16. D. Dishon, *supra* note 12, at 461.
17. *Id.* at 462.
18. Comment, *The Question of Palestinian Statehood,* 7 California Western International Law Journal 458 n. 16.
19. M. Adams, *supra* note 8, at 42.
20. *Id.*
21. *Id.* at 43.
22. *Id.* at 45.
23. *Id.* at 45.
24. Comment, *Palestinian Statehood, supra* note 18, at 458 n. 34.

12. SOME CONCLUSIONS

1. Maxine Rodinson, *Israel and the Arabs,* p. 231.
2. Elmer Berger in I. L. Kenen et al., *A Just Peace in the Middle East: How Can It Be Achieved?* p. 54.
3. Charles Douglas-Home, *The Arabs and Israel,* p. 105.
4. Eisenhower quoted in Ralph H. Magnus, ed., *Documents on the Middle East,* p. 171.
5. William V. O'Brien, *International Law and the Outbreak of War in the Middle East,* 11 Orbis 716 (1967).
6. M. Charif Bassiouni, *The Middle East: The Misunderstood Conflict,* 19 Kansas Law Review 394 (1971).

7. Washington Post, Oct. 8, 1973, sec. A, p. 13; E. Dmitriyev, *Middle East: Dangerous Tension Must Go,* International Affairs (Moscow) July 7, 1973, p. 30.

8. Quoted in Mehdi Zentar, *Statement before the Security Council,* 10 United Nations Monthly Chronicle 31 (July 1973).

9. Amos Shapira, *The Security Council Resolution of November 22, 1967: Its Legal Nature and Implications,* 4 Israeli Law Review 235 (1969).

10. John Scali, *Statement before the General Assembly,* 69 Department of State Bulletin 270 (Aug. 20, 1973).

11. Semar Seni, *Statement before the Security Council,* 9 United Nations Monthly Chronicle 22 (June 1972).

12. Quoted in Arie Bober, ed., *The Other Israel,* p. 161.

13. Elias Sam'o and Cyrus Elahi, *Resolution 242 and Beyond,* The Arab World, Aug / Sept 1971, p. 35.

14. Arnold Toynbee, *Reflections on the Crisis,* in *Reflections on the Middle East Crisis,* ed. Herbert Mason, pp. 193-94.

15. New York Times, Oct. 9, 1973, p. 44.

16. Uri Avnery, *The Third Year of the Six Days War,* in *Reflections on the Middle East Crisis,* ed. Herbert Mason, p. 157.

17. Mohammed H. El-Zayyat, *The Situation in the Middle East,* p. 14.

18. Fred J. Khouri, *The Arab-Israeli Dilemma,* pp. 318-19.

19. Avnery, *supra* note 16, at 162.

20. Quincy Wright, *The Middle East Problem,* 64 American Journal of International Law 272 (1970); Khouri, *supra* note 18, at 351.

21. Sam'o and Elahi, *supra* note 13.

22. Dean Rusk, *The 25th United Nations General Assembly and the Use of Force,* 2 Georgia Journal of International and Comparative Law 28 (1972).

13. THE ROAD TO PEACE AND THE REMAINING OBSTACLES

1. M. Adams, *The Arab-Israeli Confrontation,* 1967-78, in *The Middle East and North Africa* (1977-78).

2. *Id.*

3. Wall Street Journal, Mar. 26, 1979, p. 2, col. 3.

4. *Facts on File,* vol. 39, no. 2003, Mar. 30, 1979, at 223.

5. *Id.*

6. *Id.*

7. *Id.*

Bibliography

BOOKS

Abu-Lughod, Ibrahim, ed. *The Arab-Israeli Confrontation of June 1967: An Arab Perspective.* Evanston, Ill.: Northwestern University Press, 1970.

American Friends Service Committee. *The Search for Peace in the Middle East.* New York: Hill and Wang, 1970.

Bober, Arie, ed. *The Other Israel: The Radical Case Against Zionism.* Garden City, N.Y.: Doubleday and Co., 1972.

Burdette, Winston. *Encounter with the Middle East.* New York: Atheneum, 1969.

Dib, George, and Jabber, Faud. *Israel's Violation of Human Rights in the Occupied Territories.* Beirut: Institute for Palestine Studies, 1970.

Dodd, C. H., and Sales, M. E. *Israel and the Arab World.* New York: Barnes and Noble, 1970.

Douglas-Home, Charles. *The Arabs and Israel.* Chester Springs, Pa.: Dufour Editions, 1968.

Elkordy, Abdul-Hafez M. *Crisis of Diplomacy: The Three Wars—and After.* San Antonio, Tex.: The Naylor Co., 1971.

El-Zayyat, Mohammed H. *The Situation in the Middle East* (pamphlet). New York: Egyptian Mission to the United Nations, 1973.

Feinberg, Nathan. *The Arab-Israeli Conflict in International Law.* Jerusalem: Magnus Press, 1970.

Fisher, Roger. *Dear Israelis, Dear Arabs.* New York: Harper and Row, 1972.

Greenspan, Morris. *The Modern Law of Land Warfare.* Los Angeles: University of California Press, 1959.

Israeli Ministry for Foreign Affairs. *Facts About Israel.* Jerusalem: Division of Information, Ministry for Foreign Affairs, 1973.

———. *The Meaning of Secure Borders* (pamphlet). Tel Aviv: United Co., 1973.

Kaufmann, Myron S. *The Coming Destruction of Israel.* New York: New American Library, 1970.

Kenen, I. L.; Berger, Elmer; Pollack, Allen; and Mayhew, Christopher.

A Just Peace in the Mideast: How Can It Be Achieved? Washington, D.C.: American Enterprise Institute for Public Policy Research, 1971.

Khouri, Fred J. *The Arab-Israeli Dilemma.* Syracuse, N.Y.: Syracuse University Press, 1968.

Mason, Herbert, ed. *Reflections on the Middle East Crisis.* Paris: Mouton and Co., 1970.

Rodinson, Maxine. *Israel and the Arabs.* Translated by Michael Perl. New York: Pantheon Books, 1968.

Safran, Nadav. *From War to War: The Arab-Israeli Confrontation, 1948-1967.* New York: Pegasus, 1969.

Stone, Julius. *Legal Controls of International Conflict,* 2nd ed. New York: Rinehart and Co., 1959.

Teveth, Shabtai. *The Cursed Blessing.* New York: Random House, 1970.

Waines, David. *The Unholy War.* Wilmette, Ill.: Medina University Press International, 1971.

Wright, Quincy. *The Middle East: Prospects for Peace.* Edited by Isaac Shapiro. Dobbs Ferry, New York: Oceana Publications, 1969.

PERIODICAL LITERATURE

Bassiouni, M. Charif. *The Middle East: The Misunderstood Conflict.* 19 Kansas Law Review 394 (1971).

________. *The Middle East in Transition.* 4 The International Lawyer 383 (Jan. 1970).

Bowett, Derek. *Reprisals Involving Recourse to Armed Force.* 66 American Journal of International Law 1 (1972).

Carnegie Endowment for International Peace. *Issues before the 25th General Assembly.* 1970 International Conciliation no. 571, p. 14.

________. *Issues before the 26th General Assembly.* 1971 International Conciliation no. 584, p. 36.

Dinstein, Dr. Yoram. *The Arab-Israeli Crisis: Legal Issues and Possible Solutions.* 4 The International Lawyer 377 (Jan. 1970).

Dmitriyev, E. *Middle East: Dangerous Tension Must Go.* International Affairs (Moscow), July 7, 1973, p. 30.

El-Farra, Muhammed H. *The Role of the United Nations vis-à-vis the Palestine Question.* 33 Law and Contemporary Problems 71 (1968).

Gerson, Allen. *Trustee-Occupant: The Legal Status of Israel's Presence in the West Bank.* 14 Harvard International Law Journal 4 (1973).

Golden, Howard. *International Legal Solutions to the Middle East Crisis.* 6 The International Lawyer 5-6 (July 1972).

Halderman, John W. *Symposium: The Middle East Crisis—Test of International Law.* 33 Law and Contemporary Problems 1 (winter 1968).

Hargrove, John Lawrence. *Abating the Middle East Crisis through the United Nations (and Vice Versa).* 19 Kansas Law Review 366 (1971).

Kamenshine, Robert D. *Peacekeeping and Peacemaking—The United Nations in the Middle East.* 1 The Vanderbilt International 14 (winter-spring 1967-68).

Levine, Alan. *The Status of Sovereignty in East Jerusalem and the West Bank.* 5 New York Journal of International Law and Politics 485 (winter 1972).

Moore, John Norton. *The Arab-Israeli Conflict and the Obligation to Pursue Peaceful Settlement of International Disputes.* 19 Kansas Law Review 425 (1971).

Murphy, John F. *Symposium: The Middle East Crisis.* 19 Kansas Law Review 362 (spring 1971).

O'Brien, William V. *International Law and the Outbreak of War in the Middle East.* 11 Orbis 714 (1967).

Peretz, Don. *Israel's Administration and Arab Refugees.* 46 Foreign Affairs 336 (1968).

Piper, Donald C. *The Legal Control of the Use of Force and the Definition of Aggression.* 2 Georgia Journal of International and Comparative Law (1972).

Rosenne, Shabtai. *Directions for a Middle East Settlement.* 33 Law and Contemporary Problems 44 (1968).

Sam'o, Elias, and Elahi, Cyrus. *Resolution 242 and Beyond.* The Arab World, Aug. / Sept. 1971, pp. 32-35.

Scali, John. *Address before the General Assembly.* 69 Department of State Bulletin 270 (Aug. 20, 1973).

Shapira, Amos. *The Security Council Resolution of November 22, 1967: Its Legal Nature and Implications.* 4 Israel Law Review 229 (1969).

________. *The Six-Day War and the Right of Self Defense.* 6 Israel Law Review 68 (1971).

Stone, Julius. *The November Resolution and Middle East Peace: Pitfall or Guidepost.* 1971 University of Toledo Law Review 47.

8 United Nations Monthly Chronicle 3 (Feb. 1971).

8 United Nations Monthly Chronicle 30 (Oct. 1971).

9 United Nations Monthly Chronicle 92 (Jan. 1972).

9 United Nations Monthly Chronicle 65 (Feb. 1972).

9 United Nations Monthly Chronicle 22 (June 1972).

10 United Nations Monthly Chronicle 5 (July 1973).

Wright, Quincy. *Legal Aspects of the Middle East Situation.* 33 Law and Contemporary Problems 24 (1968).

_______. *The Middle East Problem.* 64 American Journal of International Law 270 (1970).

REFERENCE BOOKS

British Broadcasting Monitoring Service. *Summary of World Broadcasts: Part 4—The Middle East and Africa.* Jan. 22, 1973. p. A / 1.

British Broadcasting Monitoring Service. *Summary of World Broadcasts: Part 4—The Middle East and Africa.* Feb. 6, 1973, p. A / 1.

British Broadcasting Monitoring Service. *Summary of World Broadcasts: Part 4—The Middle East and Africa.* Feb. 9, 1973, p. A / 1.

British Broadcasting Monitoring Service. *Summary of World Broadcasts: Part 4—The Middle East and Africa.* Feb. 12, 1973, p. A / 1.

British Broadcasting Monitoring Service. *Summary of World Broadcasts: Part 4—The Middle East and Africa.* Feb. 14, 1973, p. A / 7.

Facts on File 1971. Jan. 1-6, 1971, pp. 9, 10.

Facts on File 1971. Feb. 4-10, 1971, p. 85.

Facts on File 1971. Feb. 11-17, 1971, p. 103.

Facts on File 1971. March 11-17, 1971, p. 181.

Facts on File 1971. April 8-14, 1971, p. 263.

Facts on File 1971. Dec. 9-15, 1971, p. 965.

Facts on File 1972. Jan. 30-Feb. 5, 1972, p. 69.

Facts on File 1972. Oct. 22-28, 1972, p. 841.

DOCUMENTS

Hearings on the Middle East Conflict before the Subcomm. on the Near East of the House Comm. on Foreign Affairs House of Representatives, 92nd Cong., 1st Sess., Doc. Y 4. F 76/1: Ea 7/10, Aug. 3, 1971.

Hearings on Approaches to Peace in the Middle East before the Subcomm. on the Near East of the Comm. on Foreign Affairs House of Representatives, 92nd Cong., 2nd Sess., Doc Y 4. F 76/1:M 58/4, Feb. 22 and 24, 1972.

Magnus, Ralph H., ed. *Documents on the Middle East,* Washington, D.C.: American Enterprise Institute for Public Policy Research, 1969.

United Nations General Assembly Resolution 2625 (xxv-1970) Doc. a/RES/2625 (xxv).

Index